Digital Voices

RESEARCH IN CREATIVE WRITING

Series Editors:

Janelle Adsit (Humboldt State University, USA)
Conchitina Cruz (University of the Philippines)
James Ryan (University of Wisconsin-Madison, USA)

Showcasing the most innovative research and field-defining scholarship surrounding Creative Writing Studies, *Research in Creative Writing* strives to discuss and demonstrate the best practices for creative writing pedagogy both inside and out of the academy. Scholarship published in the series wrestles with the core issues at the heart of the field including critical issues surrounding the practice of creative writing; multilingualism and diverse approaches to creative production; representation and the politics of aesthetics; intersectionality and addressing interlocking oppressions in and through creative writing; and the impact of teaching established lore. Responsive to emerging exigencies in the field and open to interdisciplinary and diverse contexts for creative writing, this series is designed to advance the field and push the boundaries of Creative Writing Studies. This series benefits from the guidance of and collaboration with the Creative Writing Studies Organization (https://creativewritingstudies.com/).

Titles

The Place and the Writer, edited by Marshall Moore and Sam Meekings
Craft Consciousness and Artistic Practice in Creative Writing, Ben Ristow
A-Z of Creative Writing Methods, edited by Francesca Rendle Short, Julienne Van Loon, David Carlin, Peta Murray, Stayci Taylor and Deborah Wardle

Forthcoming titles

Teaching Cultural Dexterity in Creative Writing, Micah McCrary

Related titles

Beyond Craft, Steve Westbrook and James Ryan
Imaginative Teaching, edited by Amy Ash, Michael Dean Clark and Chris Drew

Digital Voices

Podcasting in the Creative Writing Classroom

Leigh Camacho Rourks and
Saul Lemerond

BLOOMSBURY
NEW DELHI • LONDON • OXFORD • NEW YORK • SYDNEY

BLOOMSBURY INDIA
Bloomsbury Publishing India Pvt. Ltd
Second Floor, LSC Building No. 4, DDA Complex, Pocket C–6&7,
Vasant Kunj, New Delhi 110070

BLOOMSBURY, BLOOMSBURY ACADEMIC INDIA and the Diana logo are
trademarks of Bloomsbury Publishing Plc

First published in India 2025
First published in Great Britain 2023

Series design by Eleanor Rose
Cover design by Annabel Hewitson
Cover image © GarryKillian/iStock and Ali Kahfi/iStock

This edition published with permission from Bloomsbury Publishing Plc,
50 Bedford Square, London, WC1B3DP, UK

A catalogue record for this book is available from the British Library.
A catalog record for this book is available from the Library of Congress.

ISBN: 978-93-61312-88-5

For sale in the Indian subcontinent only

Series: Research in Creative Writing

Typeset by Deanta Global Publishing Services, Chennai, India
Printed and bound in India by Replika Press Pvt Ltd

To find out more about our authors and books
visit www.bloomsbury.com and sign up for our newsletters

For

Jennifer Schmidt and Lee Rourks,

Thank you

Contents

Acknowledgments

If anything is certain in this world, it is that if you know us, we have talked to you about this book. To thank everyone who has had a hand in our success or has helped the ideas in this book develop would require an acknowledgments list as long as the book itself. That said, we would like to thank all of the individual students whom we have had the pleasure of teaching at Hanover College and Beacon College. We would also like to thank all of the faculty from these institutions who have supported us as both friends and colleagues. This is, of course, also true for the students and faculty from all of the other institutions that have allowed us the privilege of working in their classrooms.

We would also like to acknowledge our three contributors, without whom the book would most certainly not have been possible. Rebecca Hazelwood, Kase Johnstun, and Billy R. Tadros are not only good friends but their expertise also was, at its most fundamental levels, necessary in this endeavor. We thank them for their ideas, enthusiasm, and their patience in allowing us to both include and edit their work.

We are also grateful to our editor, Lucy Brown, and everyone at Bloomsbury involved in this project. We are grateful for both their support and the care they put into the production of this book.

We'd also like to thank the editorial staff of the *Journal of Creative Writing Studies* for graciously granting us permission to use portions of our article, "The Virtues of Podcasting and Multimodal Literacies in the Creative Writing Classroom," published in March 2022, in this book.

Lastly, we'd like to acknowledge our families and friends as they provided us with the sort of Herculean support structures that lead us to sometimes wonder what it is we ever did to deserve them. Specifically, we'd like to thank our spouses Jennifer Schmidt and Lee Rourks.

By Saul Lemerond and Leigh Camacho Rourks

Introduction[*]

Saul Lemerond

When Leigh and I were discussing the possibility of this book, which coincidentally was the same time we were preparing an article on the same subject for the *Journal of Creative Writing Studies*, we kept returning to the question of why a book of this type did not already exist. This is not to disparage the many and varied existent works that address digital writing, digital narratives, and other hybrid works designed in and for our ever-evolving electronic landscape. The work being done to advance our understanding of how to better utilize these techniques in our classrooms is as necessary as it is amazing. But we were both drawn to podcasting, specifically, out of a shared interest in addressing a host of issues that have for too long gone unaddressed in our classrooms. This is to say that we have both been struggling for well over a decade with many problems that plague what can only be described as the "traditional" creative writing classroom. Though we know we aren't necessarily unique in this regard, it bears pointing out that our perspectives related to the teaching of creative writing have been molded by our experiences as both students and teachers of minoritized groups. Leigh Camacho Rourks is a Cuban American with a learning disability in written expression, who has, throughout her career, taught writing in institutions and programs serving significant and diverse populations of non-traditional students, probational students, at-risk youth, and currently at Beacon College, students who have

[*]Portions of this chapter first appeared in the March 2022 issue of the *Journal of Creative Writing Studies*, in our preliminary article on the subject, "The Virtues of Podcasting and Multimodal Literacies in the Creative Writing Classroom." They have since been revised and extended.

learning disabilities, ADHD, and autism spectrum disorders. I am dyslexic and have taught similarly diverse populations of students over the course of my teaching career, including at the Saginaw Chippewa Tribal College, at the University of Louisiana at Lafayette, and now, at Hanover College. Our relationship formed out of a shared interest in how multimodal learning strategies have a potential to aid in broadening the sorts of voices we tend to find in contemporary publishing, which has been stifled by mainstream, or hegemonic, cultural pressures, pressures we also see reflected in traditional writing instruction.

If you're reading this introduction, it is probably because you have noticed that podcasts could have some potential value in the creative writing classroom. Probably you've listened to a podcast before. Maybe you have one that you listen to regularly. Maybe you have several. The likelihood of this varies based on your age as well as your taste, and most certainly, your access to the internet. Chances are, though, that you do. Chances are that you listen to more than one podcast on a regular basis, and you do so for similar reasons that hundreds of millions of other people do. They are easy to listen to, and there's a lot of good ones out there. No matter what your interest is, you can find a podcast for it. Whereas until recently, the content of our media landscape was by and large controlled by a few media conglomerate gatekeepers, we're now experiencing a renaissance of artists, journalists, writers, and interviewers with the ability to forgo the traditional media barriers and reach large audiences, all with the click of a button. And while that itself is something worth noting and celebrating, we can find a good deal of optimism in the fact that the many barriers for those we call "content creators" can be tackled with just a laptop (or phone) and an internet connection. Audience and content are now a click away. This audio-medium renaissance is part of a larger artistic renaissance driven by thirty years of digital innovation, and that in and of itself would be an excellent subject of a book.

That out of all this hullabaloo we might find something valuable that we could, and by we I mean all of us, be able to apply in the creative writing classroom seems intuitive. It seems like we can find quality podcasts that exist to serve a vast prism of interests, and if this is true, then there must be a way to leverage their advantages in service of our students. There must be. The medium is too versatile for there not to be, and we've certainly approached this book with that in mind. Podcasts are cool. They are very popular, and they offer a new and dynamic landscape with which creatives can engage. And that's why we titled the book *Digital Voices*. As a general rule what you listen to when you listen to a podcast are voices. Those voices are digitally recorded, uploaded to a server in digital form, and that information is downloaded to laptops and tablets and phones, and the programs at every step of this process understand this information purely as a sequence of ones and zeros. It's awesome, really. But we are considering much more than this when we use the term "voice."

If you have spent any amount of time in a creative writing classroom, the probability is very high that you've witnessed the instructor mention (or witnessed yourself mention) that within the realm of the written word there is a thing we call "voice" and that thing is important because it's what makes any given writer unique and compelling. "What a strong voice they have," we say to our class when we go through examples of writers we wish them to learn from. We tell our students that they must develop their own voice. We tell them that it's something they need to actively think about and work on and evolve, perhaps like a Pokémon. We give our writing students the impression that if they work on their voices hard enough, and for long enough, they will have achieved that which we all desire, a "unique voice." Moreover, and not so desirable, we often discuss issues of voice with our students as though they do not already have a voice, or if they do have a voice, that it is not good enough. This is a problem. One with which the contributors to this book are at constant odds.

There can be very little argument that, generally, creative writing workshops are structured in a way that caters to mainstream cultural attitudes. For a long time this attitude skewed toward white and male because, for a long time, creative writing classrooms were predominately taught by white male professors who were instructing white male students who wished to prepare work that would then be sent out to publishers, who were also predominately white and male and straight and neurotypical, with feet (most often) set firmly in the upper-middle and upper classes. It is not as though this problem has gone away, and there are many who have pointed out that the fact that the viewpoints of writers from this demographic, viewpoints that represent a very narrow understanding of the world, preclude the perspectives of all sorts of people. And that's a damn shame. Worse, it does damage to our students. Our academic institutions are, and have for some time been, filled with such a diverse group of students that it makes very little sense to ask students to produce work with a perspective not their own, not unique, not broadening our literary landscape beyond the expected. Even in the creative writing classroom's most basic structure where a single instructor is charged with teaching a whole classroom of students, it seems almost silly to assume that this one person can hold enough acumen, and enough awareness, that we should take it as a given that they are fully fit to teach, to understand, assess, advise, and guide students who, more often than not, do not share their same worldview. It is a hard problem, and the contributors of this book do what we can to show how podcasts can be used to help face these sorts of workshop problems. Whose voices are being introduced in our creative writing classrooms? Whose voices are privileged? Whose voices are heard? If you've spent time in a creative writing classroom, you no doubt have noticed that some people's voices are heard more than others. If you've ever taken part of a traditional workshop, you probably notice that the only voice you don't get to hear is the writer's, which, ironically, happens to be the most important voice in the room because, at that moment, it's the writer's work that's being discussed.

This book is titled *Digital Voices* because voice is its focus. We are, each one of us, interested in how we can use podcasts to approach, advocate for, encourage, and lift each and every voice in our classrooms. And, because podcasting is such a diverse medium, our approaches are diverse as well.

So here, we will strive to answer a simple question: Why should we incorporate podcasts into the creative writing classroom? We will point out how the value of podcasting is apparent given its place in our culture as arguably the most popular and fastest-growing form of media. We will also discuss how it provides a number of pedagogical benefits for creative writing students and creative writing instructors alike. For instance, we will discuss the value of creating podcasts as a multimodal and metacognitive creative exercise that puts students' voices at the forefront of their stories. For those who are unfamiliar, the term "multimodal" refers to the mode in which communicated language is both related and understood, for instance the written word as a mode differs from that of spoken language (also a mode) which differs from the communication that we see in gestures (another mode) which also differs in certain respects from visual representations (again, a mode). The term "metacognitive" refers to the act of thinking about your thinking. In practice, metacognitive learning involves teachers asking their students to think, "How and why *am I* learning," while they are learning.

There's a lot that's been written about both multimodal literacy and metacognitive learning, which is a softer way of saying that it has a rich academic literature. And there is a case to be made that centering the discussion on multimodality can prove valuable, especially considering how much of the framework for multimodal pedagogy lives within the realm of multicultural literacies. We are especially concerned by the ways that workshops and singular modality creative writing classes fail to serve a considerable portion of students, either because they do not feel welcome or because they do not feel capable. That being said, it would seem that podcasts exist within an *a priori* cultural space, almost as if tailormade to address these and other prevalent questions with which those in our field currently struggle.

More than that, while it is a good thing that podcast creation affords students a multimodal, and hopefully metacognitive, learning experience, it also allows them a space in their narratives where they can more directly highlight their voices. At the same time, this helps us put focus on issues of intersectionality that not only are another matter to be considered when adapting multimodal and metacognitive theories but are also both inherent and integral to the pedagogical groundwork (or to put it another way, the framework of teaching, or the scaffolding) that supports it. This is because, as much of the field of study suggests, if multimodal and metacognitive learning is valuable because it allows students to increase the number of connections they make to the content which they are studying, then one must assume that the student's identity is fundamental to that process, that is, it is their ability to personally identify with both creative instruction and the material creative process that allows them to understand and internalize what it is they're learning. It would perhaps be an understatement to say that, ideally, this should allow for increased efficiency of learning within the student. Again, if the fundamental goal is to allow students avenues to make personal connections to both the content of their creative work and their instruction, then once that groundwork (or scaffolding) has been established, students can benefit from the diverse creative perspectives of their peers as well as diverse perspectives of other writers, ultimately providing them with the ability to apply that self-knowledge to their own creative output.

As a pedagogical medium, as teaching tools, podcasts present a great deal of versatility. Since it's been established that one can make a podcast about anything, the possibility space for the sorts of projects students can be asked to take part in is vast, and frankly, this is putting it mildly. Just from the perspective of how we generally organize creative writing classrooms today, we can ask students to create poetry podcasts, narrative fiction podcasts, creative nonfiction podcasts, and interview podcasts. This is to say that there is no potential focus of study or issue that is prevalent in our classrooms that we could not ask students to create a podcast about. And, while Leigh and I found, and continue to find this incredibly exciting, and have made, and continue to make great efforts to incorporate many of these ideas into our classrooms, we knew other instructors who were incorporating podcasts in their creative writing classrooms in different ways. Ways that we knew to be just as exciting. So, it seemed only fitting that we reach out to these folks and asked them to contribute to this book. This is because it is our hope that our readers can get as wholistic an understanding of how and why one might consider adopting these differing approaches in their classrooms. Or perhaps more importantly, for those interested in the creative potential of podcasts to embrace that potentiality in service of both themselves and others.

We begin the book with Chapter 1, "Historical Context-Present," which is an account of the contemporary state of podcasting along with a short history of mainstream audio mediums, beginning at the dawn of broadcasting. One of the most powerful things about our current podcasting landscape is, at least at the time of writing this introduction, that the internet has provided a space with far fewer barriers to entry. In the past, if one wanted to create an audio product, what today we affectionately refer to as content, even acquiring the necessary equipment for such a thing was a daunting task. Perhaps the largest barrier was access to a radio transmitter. Something not so easy given that this was a privilege afforded to only a select few, especially considering the racist gatekeeping enforced by the Federal Communications Commission or

FCC, the structure, and effects of which are still prevalent, which is to say they can still be clearly seen in today's broadcasting industry. An industry that has, and continues to, actively exclude minoritized voices at an alarming rate. One might wonder how it is that a country as large as America can have such a diverse population yet have a disproportionately small number of diverse perspectives. Not a minor point considering just how small this number of voices still is.

That mainstream, and academic, cultural production and instruction (this is what we mean when we say, hegemony) has yet to address the damage the ignorance of this pluralism has caused is the subject of Chapter 2, "The Many Voices Classroom." Here, Leigh Camacho Rourks discusses how both considerations of creative writing workshops and instruction as it relates to the genres of fiction, poetry, and creative nonfiction need to be examined along with considerations of creative production within the classroom. She does this by pointing out glaring issues with a traditional workshop model that, since its codification in the 1920s, has not yet fully reckoned with its history. She points out how the negative power structures that assisted in its creation are still baked into its organization. She also addresses complaints that workshops consistently serve to deny, silence, erase, or otherwise discourage the lived experiences of a host of identity groups. This is, of course, very much an issue integral to using podcasts as multimodal learning platforms that strive to make sure that students' narratives, as well as the narratives of diverse groups, are heard. This is because if the fundamental pedagogical goal is to allow students avenues to make personal connections to both the content of their creative work and their instruction, then we can also argue that, once that groundwork has been established, students will be able to benefit from the diverse creative perspectives of their peers as well as diverse perspectives of other writers.

The focus here is on the learning lives of our students, and Leigh Camacho Rourks goes on to address this in Chapter 3, "Craft and Metacognition." This is because, while Leigh Camacho Rourks has for some time been incorporating a number of interview podcasts with a diverse group of writers to offer differing writing perspectives, she also asks her students to create podcasts as metacognitive exercises. Podcasts where she asks her students to talk about how it is that they think about and analyze creative work. So, in this chapter,

Leigh Camacho Rourk's dives into the theoretical, and psychologically supported, underpinnings of metacognitive exercises as they relate to craft and explains how they can be applied to the realm of podcasting. As it turns out, podcasting offers students a new level of introspection, and because it is done in service of a larger discussion, they begin to orient their own goals and progress within a more diverse literary community than they might find in their own classroom. This is especially helpful for first-generation college students and students whose backgrounds are underrepresented in workshops. Additionally, since the podcast interview hinges on prepared questions based on the interviewees work, it asks students to engage deeply both as readers and writers, testing and growing their own understanding of craft through partnership, refining it as they find ways to articulate their ideas for a larger audience, either to their fellow students when played in class or to the greater world. This purposeful reflexive exploration is an excellent path to voice and asking students to create their own metacognitive podcasts helps students travel it.

Many of these principles can be applied to Chapter 4, "Fiction: Multimodality and the Storytelling Podcast," as well. In this chapter, I argue that there's a value in asking students to create narrative podcasts specifically because it's a multimodal creative exercise that puts student's voices at the forefront of their stories. This is to say that while it is valuable that podcast creation affords students a multimodal learning experience, it also allows them a space where they can highlight their voices, placing them at the forefront of their own narratives. And I ultimately argue that issues of intersectionality are not only another matter to be considered when adapting multimodal theories to learning but also that those issues are both inherent and integral to the pedagogical groundwork that supports it. This is to say that if, as the entire field of study supports, multimodal learning is valuable because it allows students to increase the number of cognitive connections to the content which they are studying, then one must assume that the student's identity is integral to that process, that is, the ability to personally identify with both creative instruction and with the material creative process, ideally, should allow for the increased efficiency of learning within our students, and more importantly, without damaging our students' self-identity.

In Chapter 5, "Poetry: From Performance to Analysis," Billy R. Tadros addresses how we can use ideas of performance and poetry in podcasts as a way of redefining the ways in which we think about evaluating creative products that originate in our classrooms. Billy R. Tadros argues for the inclusion of podcasts in the poetry classroom as both course texts and student assignments as a way of sanctioning the notion that creativity is something common and accessible rather than, as we often imagine, "something exclusive and elite." This leads to her realization that there are a great number of prospective students outside of those select few that instructors often single out as having talent. "Talent" in this case is that which instructors recognize as writing that could possibly be successful in existing creative writing industries that have found acceptance within our profession, like MFA programs and prestigious literary journals. Billy R. Tadros also addresses how podcasts, as well as other digital technologies, have changed the ways students understand forms of writing like poetry. This is because poetry has for some time been held up by certain, often elitist, institutions. However, students today are coming into classrooms having already engaged with a good deal of poetry on social media sites like Instagram, and these relatively new digital spaces offer both student and instructor a wider understanding of what poetry is, what it can do, what makes it good, and how it is produced. She also presents several practical ways we can challenge students to think about these sorts of issues by creating podcasts. Offering best practices as well as thoughts on the possibility space that podcasts provide as teaching tools.

Rebecca Hazelwood offers similar directional insights in Chapter 6, "Creative Nonfiction: The Sound of Truth." Rebecca Hazelwood, like the rest of the contributors to this book, identifies several damaging issues found in creative writing instruction. However, she addresses how these issues are even more acute for writers of creative nonfiction as she mentions, "The traditional workshop model has never worked for writers of nonfiction." This is because creative nonfiction writers are often writing from a place of experience, writing pieces autobiographical in nature, and then are asked to remain silent while others engage in critique. This is, as one might expect, damaging. Arguably, it is more damaging to writers of creative nonfiction than it is to writers of fiction and poetry because the criticism is focused directly on the writer's personal experience. Podcasting allows students more agency, which is something one might imagine is desirable in the realm of creative nonfiction. Podcasts can also address a number of other issues in the creative nonfiction classroom. Students must edit their work and therefore listen to themselves. Listen to their own voices tell their own stories, knowing that their peers are not only going to hear these stories but also listen to the person who owns their story, tell their story. Additionally, the necessity to edit gives students more time to sit with their work. To hear themselves read it. To think about what is working and what is not. Having any voice, or number of voices, be heard is the name of the game in creative nonfiction because its scope is individual human experience in the most direct way one might imagine it. And if this is the case, a true sense of agency should be the ground on which this game is played.

Kase Johnstun holds a position that is quite unique, though hopefully not for too long, for those of us in the world of creative writing instruction. He is a creative writing instructor who has a podcast where he interviews writers, which is why we asked him to write Chapter 7, "Teacher as Podcaster." Kase Johnstun's experience interviewing a plurality of writers is in and of itself a valuable enterprise. In previous chapters many writers point out how important (so important as to be necessary) it is to introduce students to a diverse group of writing voices as issues of craft and process have never been as homogenous, or standardized, as many in our profession would have you believe. Writer-interview podcasts model this latitude for student and instructor alike. What Johnstun offers in his chapter, among many other insights, is a literal how-to for interview podcasters. He discusses the sorts of demands the form have on the interviewer as well as the demands it has on those interviewed. What follows is a celebration of writing process the results of which drive inspiration, motivation, and understanding in those who have the fortune of listening. And, of course, he not only provides guidance for creative writing instructors who might be interested in starting their own craft of writing podcasts, he makes sure to ask his students to do it as well. He asks his students to interview each other as if they were actual writers because they are actual writers. To read each other's work out loud. To ask questions about the work of the writer to the writer, and ultimately to think about what it means to be a writer doing the work of writing.

Our final two chapters—Chapter 8, "Audience and Publishing," and Chapter 9, "The Digital Divide and Podcasting"—address issues that most probably stand at the forefront of our student's minds. The reach of podcasting is great, with vast potential audiences. Who a student's potential audience is, and where they might find them are two questions most students want answered. This is not just because our students want to find a way to monetize their content as soon as they can and for as much cash as possible. Yes, many of them do, and we cannot blame them as the majority of them are young and looking for a lifetime vocation. But, at the same time, our students' motivations vary depending on what's important to them. It stands to reason that if they're writing, if they're creating, that they want their voices to be heard. Whether it is that they would like others to enjoy what they've produced, or if they have something, a cause, that they believe in. Our students are not passionless. In my experience, I've found that the opposite is true. Where to publish? How to publish? These are the first steps in reaching the sorts of communities, the sorts of conversations, they desire to take part in. The number of pedagogically sound reasons to ask students to create podcasts are many and varied and enumerated at length in the previous chapters, and we ask instructors to acknowledge the inherent value in this, but few students wish to learn for learning's sake. The digital revolution has created spaces where they can thrive, and that must at the very least be acknowledged. Success should no longer be seen as a zero-sum game between the haves and the have nots. To date myself and this introduction, there was a time when I watched reruns of *Seinfeld* every night because they were the only thing to watch. This is no longer the case. Now, if we wish to engage with a piece of content more than once it's because it's so amazing, so compelling, that we *have to* watch or listen to it again. The days of watching reruns existed because the barriers to new content were clear, which is to say it was (still is) controlled by a small number of suits at an even smaller number of networks or broadcasting agencies. And this is why Chapter 9 is also so important. If you're reading this book, there's a good chance that you exist in an academic or at least academic adjacent space. Folks like me who exist in these spaces tend to take certain things for granted. A computer, usually a laptop, maybe a tablet, maybe all of these things and more are some of those things. A dedicated internet connection is another.

It's a simple and unpleasant fact that not everyone has access to these things. There is a digital divide in this country that works to create barriers to entry that work much in the same way the old barriers to entry did. The better we understand this the better we can assist our students as well as ourselves, and Leigh Camacho Rourks asks that we take this to heart (and to head as well). Moreover, she provides guidance on how to address this in the classroom so that we can better serve our students, and so our students can become better stewards of their voices. This is because, as I hope this introduction as well as the rest of this book makes clear, the traditional creative writing classroom has for too long been a silencer of voices. And it is now more than ever that our students' voices need to be elevated.

1

Historical Context-Present (The State of the Podcast)

Saul Lemerond

Here, I intend to give a brief history of the podcast (which gets its name from Apple's first MP3 players) as it's currently understood, as well as acknowledge the narrative traditions, like that of radio, that laid the groundwork for this medium, while at the same time discussing the historical barriers that have and continue to exist for these audio mediums. Beginning with a brief summary of the state of podcasting today, and then moving on to its roots in Golden Age Radio Shows, I will relate how these traditions translate into our contemporary era. This is because there is inarguably a resurgence of audio mediums with an array of podcasting styles and forms, some in the style of radio dramas, like the incredibly popular, *Welcome to the Night Vale*, *This American Life*, and *Serial* style documentary-features, and a whole host of "Chumcasts" (or "Buddycasts"; this is where two or more hosts riff off of each other about a specified topic), like *2 Dope Queens* and *My Favorite Murder*, and of course the large number of interview podcasts like *WTF*, *Song Exploder*, and *The Joe Rogan Podcast*. In addition to acknowledging both the history and traditions of these audio mediums, I also want to discuss the ways in which podcasting offers its listeners and creators opportunities that could have never been possible during the "golden age" of radio.

In 2021, the website Spotify listed 3.2 million podcasts.[1]There are similar numbers of podcasts listed on other hosting websites like Soundcloud, Apple podcasts, Podbean, and Stitcher. I often tell my students that if they can imagine an idea for a podcast, and that podcast doesn't already exist, it means they should probably consider making one. This is because, while the number of podcasts may already seem large, the number of listeners to podcasts is much larger and growing, with both Apple and Spotify boasting a podcast listenership in excess of 28 million,[2] and the total number of podcast listeners in the hundreds of millions. It is not uncommon for today's most popular podcast audiences to exceed the audiences for major movies, television, and radio shows. And what I tell my students is true, there is seemingly a podcast for anything. There are podcasts devoted to single radio or television shows. There are podcasts devoted to bad movies, the audiences to which, most likely eclipse the viewing audiences of the movies they sometimes choose to discuss. There are fiction podcasts, fan-fiction podcasts, slash/fiction podcasts, poetry podcasts, and the list goes on and on.

The question of why podcasts are so popular, and why there are so many of them, is one of access. Podcasts are cheap, downloadable, and can be listened to while one does a host of other things like driving, cleaning, playing video games, studying, working, or just decompressing. This is a revolutionary change when compared to radio programing because that content was fixed in both a time and a place, which is to say that consumers were beholden to whatever was on-air at any given time. For many radio listeners, or TV watchers, an on-air programing schedule became normalizing background noise to those who listened to or watched them. Whether it's cable news, daily soaps, talk radio, or your favorite old, syndicated TV show, or, as is the case with many listeners of radio, just music. The digital age has altered this completely. The option of streaming or downloading digital content has changed the average person's daily life in that they are now unbeholden to content that's "the best of what's on," which is to say that, if one can stream or download what they want, when they want, then they can be far more discerning concerning the whats, whens, and wheres, of content consumption. This is most likely why Netflix produced and released 371 titles in 2019.[3] It's true that many people probably still want to put *Friends* on in the background while they fold their laundry; however, there is a greater and greater desire among consumers to watch new shows that fit their specific tastes.[4]

There is, of course, a difference between an audio streaming service that hosts podcasting content, like Spotify or Soundcloud, and a video streaming service like Netflix, which mostly relies on producing its own content. This is to say that no one posts their content on Netflix's service for free. Netflix doesn't allow that. Instead, for the most part, Netflix greenlights and produces its own content (which coincidentally, now includes podcasts). In 2020, the service told its investors that it planned to spend 17 billion dollars developing new content.[5]

On the other hand, most of the content that appears on Soundcloud or Stitcher is made by creators independent of the hosting site, who then make that content available to their users for free. There are, of course, exceptions to this as many of these sites hide some, or in the case of Spotify, much of their content behind a paywall. One might wonder why it is that Netflix must spend 17 billion dollars a year on content, which amounts to about 400 new titles, and a website that hosts podcasts, like Spotify, can spend 340 million dollars a year on its content, or even more interestingly, a website like Stitcher or Soundcloud can spend almost nothing on them at all in relative terms and still boast user bases of over a hundred million.[6]

The answer is that these sites allow anyone to post their podcast on them for free. So, while Netflix must hire production companies to greenlight scripts, hire actors and directors, and sound and film editors, as well as wardrobe and makeup, scout locations, and then shoot its content, Soundcloud does none of that. Anyone who wants to make a podcast can make their podcast, and Soundcloud will host it so long as the podcast doesn't violate the terms of its user agreement. Still, one might ask, how can it be, even then, that while Netflix can spend 17 billion dollars on new content and get 370 new shows as a result, Spotify can spend what amounts to 7 percent of that and add 1.3 million new podcasts? Don't those podcasts also need production companies and producers and editors and voice talent, whether they're actors or simply professional talkers? Shouldn't there be agents involved? Don't they need studios? Don't those studios need techs and editors? As of 2021, Spotify had 2.2 million podcasts which means there's got to be a lot of studios, techs, and sound editors out there.[7] How is it that we aren't constantly driving past studios on our way to the grocery store? It's simple, the vast majority of these podcasts are made by independent creators who have taught themselves what they need to know in order to make the content they want. Are there podcasts that are professionally made? Sure, plenty of them are, though it's worth pointing out that many of the popular professionally produced podcasts of today didn't start off that way. They started off like most podcasts do. One or more people with an idea recorded themselves executing that idea, edited that recording, and then put it on the internet.

This DIY (do-it-yourself), self-taught mindset toward creating content combined with offering that content free at the point of access is revolutionary, and it's incredibly important for a whole host of reasons. Both recently and historically, radio, film, and television were mediums with very narrow points of access for those who wanted to break into the industry. For a very long time, the number of radio frequencies, television channels, and feet of film were scarce resources. The people with access to those frequencies, channels, and feet of film were the producers and programmers who controlled the stream of content. Radio stations have owners, so do TV channels. If you want your content to reach that medium, you need to convince the gatekeepers, the people with access to that medium, that your art, or your content, is the sort of content they want, and these are the sort of cultural choke points that have long kept underserved and underrepresented communities underrepresented and underserved.

Audio Mediums: Radio and Podcast

I teach a course titled, "Creative Writing and the Podcast." It is not uncommon for students in the beginning of the course, when we discuss the fiction (or the storytelling) podcast, to ask me, what's the difference between a storytelling podcast and a radio play? Or, if they are creating a creative nonfiction podcast, they often want to know what the difference is between a docu-feature style podcast and a docu-feature style radio show like *This American Life*? Nearly all of them want to know what the difference is between a radio program and a podcast. To them, and to everyone, they sound nearly identical. However, there are distinct differences that exist between them that make delineation important. What they have in common, in fact, is that they are both audio mediums. Considering them as interchangeable detracts from a large number of diverging factors, many having to do with access (both on the side of the creators and the end user) in terms of logistics, content, availability, and scarcity.

Radio as we understand it today began in 1894 with the invention of the radio transmitter/receiver. At the time, this device operated by transmitting sound across radio waves which have always existed as part of the electromagnetic spectrum. Interestingly enough, all of the wireless communication technologies we use today use these same radio waves, from smartphones to Roku televisions to wireless routers to orbiting satellites. All of these devices operate off of a set of waves theorized by James Clark Maxwell in 1867, which were then experimentally demonstrated to exist by Heinrich Hertz in 1887, and then practically put into use by Guglielmo Marconi in 1894 with the invention of the first practical radio transmitter.[8] The first radios were used for peer-to-peer communication. Basically, allowing personal communication between two or more people over distance. This communication would be done over a single frequency between two people that were in range of one another's transmitters. If two people were trying to broadcast over the same frequency, the broadcaster with the more powerful transmitter would be heard and the person with the less powerful transmitter would not. This is important because it means that radio frequencies can be placed into two categories: (1) They are, like air and water, considered part of "the public commons," and (2) They are scarce, which is to say only one person can broadcast over a single range of frequency at a time. As more and more people began to own radios, the temptation to simply tune across the different frequencies and listen to others became strong. With this came the desire for frequencies dedicated to specific public purposes, namely news and other informative broadcasts and entertainment.

From the time that the first radio transmitter was developed, anyone with a radio transmitter could broadcast whatever they wanted on whatever frequency they wanted to whomever else had a radio receiver within their broadcast distance. In the United States, anyone could do it on any frequency they wanted until, beginning with the 1912 Radio Act, the United States created a legal structure regulated by government bodies like the Federal Communications Commission (FCC), which then required licensure for any entity to be granted permission to transmit over large swaths of bandwidth.[9] After the Radio Act, which would later be amended with the formation of the FCC, broadcast stations were required to be licensed by the federal government, with a narrow bandwidth allotment for amateur radio broadcasters. It is also the genesis of broadcasting networks, CBS and ABC being among them.

It is nearly impossible to overstate how revolutionary radios were in the realm of communication. Isolated farming communities would use them to keep up on current events in near real time. They had access to real-time fluctuating price indices of their goods. The entire country used radios to keep themselves updated on the war efforts. Radios were perhaps even more revolutionary in the realm of art and entertainment because now, for the first time, various shows could be brought into the home, a space that heretofore had been dominated by table games, music, talk, and literature, or some combination thereof. By the 1920s there were radios in a large number of American households. By 1947, 82 percent of Americans listened to radio.[10] The 1920s to 1940s came to be considered the Golden Age of Radio. And there was a mad dash among programmers to find a way to translate as many popular forms of entertainment to the medium as possible (this same phenomenon would be repeated for television in the following decades). It is during the Golden Age of Radio that we see the development of, and this list is by no means exhaustive, radio plays, situational comedies, mystery serials, soap operas, variety and talent shows, quiz shows, sports, children's and cooking shows. This is the era of the *Lone Ranger*, *Amos and Andy*, *The Shadow*, *Jack Benny*, and *Gracie Allen*.

Many of these shows are based off of the sorts of shows one might go to a theater, or some other form of physical venue, to see. As I alluded to earlier, all of this art and entertainment had to be selected by station programmers and then produced for a mass audience. This is significant for many reasons, but it's significant for our discussion on podcasting as it marks a major barrier for creators that has existed for a long time. Probably the largest barrier for creators who wanted to broadcast their content was access to a transmitter. Especially if one did not have the personal ability to buy or build a transmitter. The longer the range, the larger potential audience you wanted, the bigger your transmitter needed to be, the more expensive it would be to build and maintain. If you wanted to broadcast, you needed a license to broadcast across a specific frequency for a specific distance. This is an issue of money and resources, and if you did not have them, you had to find someone who did, and even after that you needed a license to use the airwaves. So, another barrier comes in obtaining a license to broadcast from the FCC. The third being that, if you didn't have your own station, you needed to be hired and approved by a programmer for a station that did have a license. And, after all of that, your program content needed to be approved by the FCC, which has certain standards for what is appropriate to broadcast across the airwaves. Radio scholar Richard Berry explains it this way:

> Historically, commercial radio programming is safe, inoffensive and mass market to maintain advertisers and to build and maintain the largest possible audience. To programmers this is consistency, whereas to audiences it is predictability. MacFarland describes this philosophy as the McDonaldization of radio with predictability and familiarity being building factors in programming strategy. It could be argued (and evidence of student listening bears this out) that it is predictability in commercial radio that has created the fall in listening by the "wirefree" generation and the movement of audiences (in the UK) from commercial radio to BBC national radio or to streaming web stations and Podcasts.[11]

"Safe, inoffensive and mass market" by definition and implication, must tow the main line of hegemonic discourse. This is true for television as well. It is a consequence of a limited number of bandwidths that control the entirety of possible consumable content across that medium. There are only so many choices, and those choices must abide by the standards of the FCC as well as appeal to the largest, most homogenous, audience possible. Today, the number of radio stations, or even television channels, one might have access to is larger than it has ever been in the past. This, however, does not ease the difficulty in starting and maintaining a station, let alone a show that might live on that station. Even if one has the money, the staff, and the acumen to start their own radio station, they're still limited in audience size by the strength of their transmitter as well as limited in terms of content. This is to say nothing of the massive systemic barriers to entry that have and continue to exist for much of minoritized America.

The racist history of the FCC has been well documented, and it perhaps should come as no surprise that while there is an implicit barrier to any economically disadvantaged community to radio licensure, there is also an explicitly racist one as the FCC has an admitted, and documented, history of denying minoritized groups licensure, though it should be noted that this is particularly and especially true for African Americans.[12] So, while there is an economic sense in which radio stations need to be "safe and inoffensive" to be profitable, there is also a very real, and very overt, history in which people were denied licensure because of their race, the effects of which continue to this day.

As one might imagine, these barriers to licensure served to restrict access to the radio waves, and the audience of those radio waves by consequence, for a whole host of people for a whole host of reasons. This is further complicated by the limited nature of bandwidth as a resource, and while one can assume that nearly any person lying in the margins of the hegemonic cultural discourse would continue to be marginalized in this venture similar to the ways they are marginalized in others, recorded history bears this out in stark relief. This is especially true for race. David Honig, in an article in the *Southern Law Review*, points out that "It is no accident that 88 years after the FCC's birth, when 38.7% of Americans are persons of color, minority television ownership stands at 2.6% and is dropping fast, and minority radio ownership is stagnant at about 5%."[13] This is because well into the 1950s, zero minorities owned radio stations, and the FCC proceeded to grant very few licenses to minorities in the decades that followed.[14] The reasons for this is the FCC would not grant licensure to minorities, stating in its guidelines for licensure that stations must serve "the general public good." The stated "reasoning" behind the denial of licensure was that the FCC believed that minority-owned radio stations would cater to minority audiences, which by their analysis was "too narrow an audience" to serve the general public good. This logic was even extended, at times, to white-owned radio stations that scheduled Black-oriented programming. What compounds this problem is that even though the FCC acknowledges its past of systemic discrimination, it's done little to remedy it. The reason remedy is an issue is because, since there are only a finite number of bandwidths that the FCC can provide a license, and since the FCC had already granted licensure of most of the relevant bandwidths to white-owned stations by the time it decided to recognize and reverse its policies, there are now far fewer possible licenses to grant. And the FCC has, for the most part, refused to grant preferences for minority ownership. What is even more astonishing is that they continued to enact licensure guidelines that penalized minority applicants. A 2000 study done by the FCC found that minority applicants had a lower probability to obtain a license because "The most commonly invoked attributes were 'past broadcast experience' dating to 1936 and 'past broadcast record,' dating to 1954." As the FCC well knew, virtually no minorities could have shown "past broadcast experience" because almost no broadcasters hired minorities; and virtually no minorities could have shown "past broadcast record" because the FCC wasn't issuing any licenses to minorities.[15]

This is compounded even more so by the fact that existing stations, because they did not have to worry about counter-programming against minority content from minority-owned stations, were not incentivized to add minority content into their lineups.[16] I'll state later in the chapter that podcasting is superior to radio if only for the reason that it doesn't have this specific systemic barrier to entry. That's not to say that podcasting has no systemic barriers, it does, it's just that they are not as starkly bleak as they seem to be in the realm of radio and television broadcasting.

Content Restrictions

So, not putting aside the barriers that exist for people with a desire to just be on the radio at all, there is also the issue of content restrictions. So even if you have access to a transmitter, and the FCC has granted licensure, and the station itself (if you don't own it yourself) has decided it values the content that you produce, you still need to make sure your work abides by FCC content guidelines. And, if the content restrictions of the FCC and the station don't automatically preclude your content from appearing in the first place, then there is also a good chance that those restrictions will eventually end up limiting, dictating, and/or compromising the sort of content that you create.

The FCC has restrictions against radio content that it deems obscene, profane, or indecent. Regardless of this, there are also natural restrictions on content in terms of audience appeal, like Berry alluded to earlier. This is to say that if you have content that appeals to a number of people, but that number of people isn't large enough to move the ratings needle, then you're not going to get your content on air. Thus, perhaps the largest content restriction is that your work, whatever it may be, must appeal to enough people in the listening area to make it attractive to advertisers, which means that shows with more selective, smaller audiences have difficulty finding purchase within that landscape given the demographic and economic demands of the market, which again is just another way of saying that the content must conform to the dictates of cultural homogeneity. This is perhaps why one can turn the radio to any station and know instantly the sort of show they're listening to, which is to say that if a station is not a music station, then it is most likely a station devoted to sports or politics, with the occasional shock or comedy show. Most of whom do the best job they can at reenforcing the marginalizing norms of our society.

All of this is to say that if one took the possible number of content creators and then tried to fit them into the radio landscape, you would have something that looked like a pyramid that grew ever narrower, and with a vanishingly small number of people actually making it on-air in any capacity. It is interesting that the docu-style audio broadcast, for example, *This American Life* is perhaps one of the most popular style of podcasts. There are easily thousands if not tens of thousands of them, but for some reason few other radio stations were willing, or successful, in creating their own style of show of this type. However, somehow podcasters are able to do it regularly. Even NPR has been able to do it with podcasts in a way it was never able to do with its scheduled radio lineup.[17]But NPR aside, one of the most compelling reasons independent podcasters are able to do this is that *anyone* can currently make a reasonable living through podcasting by cultivating a subscriber base on Patreon. This is a point I'll be repeating later because it bears repeating.

Even more excitingly, the freedom and autonomy afforded by the medium goes both ways, which is to say both creator and consumer benefit. For the sake of argument, let's say that there is an enjoyable radio program out there that by serendipity is perfectly tailored to your tastes. If the show does not air during a time when you are available to listen to it, the show itself, though apparently perfect in a way that only you could appreciate, could just as well not exist in the first place. Many people listen to the radio for many reasons, but very few people make it a point to listen to the radio every waking hour of every day.

The New Audio Medium

The first recorded use of the word "Podcasting," a portmanteau, came from Ben Hammersley of the *Guardian* who suggested that the word be used to describe an iPod broadcast. One way podcasting has been classified is "as a technology used to distribute, receive, and listen, on-demand, to sound content produced by traditional editors such as radio, publishing houses, journalists, and educational institutions . . . as well as content created by independent radio producers, artists, and radio amateurs."[18] The assumption of radio content is perhaps erroneous, though understandable. The operative words of this definition are "on-demand . . . sound produced by traditional editors . . . as well as . . . amateurs." As mentioned before there are a number of radio platforms that also post their programs as podcasts, though, as this section will explain, the experience of them as podcasts makes them fundamentally different. Scholar David Black noted that the definition and understanding of podcasts may be ultimately linked given the public's general understanding of the two mediums:

> Listeners have a lot to do with it. A medium's identity stems in part from how it is received and treated by its users. Listeners may of course be nudged in this or that direction by the industry. But if, for whatever reason,

> Internet audio is treated as if it were radio, then to some irreducible extent it is radio.[19]

However, it is important to discuss some distinctions between traditional radio broadcasts and podcasts as what makes podcasts distinct is a very large part of what makes them a revolutionary medium

The beginnings of podcasting, and of serial content, blogging and otherwise, came in from software developers Dave Winer and Adam Curry who wrote the programing for what is now known as an RSS feed. RSS feeds provide a link between the creators and the user. All any creator needs is a hosting site, and if anyone who for any reason becomes interested in the creator's content and wants to subscribe so that they can get it regularly, all they have to do is link to their RSS feed and that user will be updated whenever the creator's RSS feed is updated. This technology has revolutionized media in so many ways, and so completely that it would take another whole book to address them. To put it simply, the RSS feed allows users to sign up for as many different creator's content as they want, and the program feed enables them to be notified whenever new content has been uploaded onto the host's platform. Curry notes, "I like the fact that people were starting to blog audio files, but I didn't want to go have look for them [*sic*]. I wanted a magical experience."

This is where the issue of access becomes revealing. For traditional radio, the barriers to access, whether they are issues of economics, wavelength scarcity, racism, state censorship, demand, or availability, dramatically restrict opportunities for creators to reach an audience, and even they aren't able to reach an audience at all with content authentic to their creative interests. Internet access, RSS feeds, and free personal recording and editing software have virtually eliminated most of these barriers to entry. To make a podcast, all a person needs is a concept and a script, recording and editing software (both of which are available for free on the internet), a hosting site (which one can obtain for free, at least for a little while) and an RSS feed link. It should be noted that most website templates for website builders like WIXX, Squarespace, or Go Daddy already come with RSS feed software built into them.

To listen to a podcast, all you need to do is subscribe and download the podcast onto your device. Previously, radio station producers and programmers controlled when, how, and who you'd listen to. Now the user gets to decide who they want to listen to and when. Berry notes how important this is:

> Once on a player, listeners can mix various Podcasts with their own music to create their own playlist of content. The listener is now in charge of the broadcast schedule choosing what to listen to, when, in what order and—perhaps most significantly—where. Although the producers still maintain control over content, the listeners make decisions over scheduling and the listening environment and that is a fundamental change for producers of radio content.[20]

This is how you end up with sites like Spotify hosting 2.2 million podcasts to audiences of over one hundred million people. Because of subscription service websites like Patreon, podcasters are able to monetize their content in ways that incentivizes many of them to continue producing content. Social media platforms have made it as easy as ever for creators to promote tailored content to small but interested groups of people, with the potential to grow if they feel they could have, or want to have, mass market appeal. The concept behind Patreon is fairly simple, journalist Dave Johnson writes, "Patreon is a membership platform that connects content creators with fans and supporters. Mainly, it offers financial tools that let supporters subscribe to projects that give creators a predictable income stream as they continue to create content." Subscriptions are generally anywhere from $1 to $10 per month or per content creation. This allows creators an alternative method to the more mainstream demands of the airwaves, the selective barriers to which have already been discussed.

The function of Patreon, and sites like it, also leads us to another major difference between radio and podcasting. Patrons are paying the creators directly, and in cases where creators have a relatively low number of subscribers, like 100 or even 1,000, the connection between the user and the creator can often feel much more intimate. This concept of intimacy, or at the very least, closeness that often exists between podcasters and their listeners doesn't just stop there. Scholar Mia Lindgren notes that audio mediums tend to have a personalizing effect on listeners: "Radio and podcast storytelling is perfectly placed to explore lived, personal experiences. Unlike stories produced for screens where emotions are acted out in visual form, audio stories (readily available on smartphones) explore our lives through sounds and spoken words, intimately whispered into our ears."[21] What Lindgren is describing has a long history of study, mostly due to the popularity among academics to the NPR show *This American Life*, and then later with the breakout NPR hit podcast *Serial*. For Lindgren, the contemporary experience of listening to audio mediums of storytelling is probably amplified by what seems to be the most preferred delivery system for them, headphones (and/or earbuds). The idea is that headphones have a way of isolating the user, leading to a more personalized experience, which leads us to the claim that "Podcasts represent an atomization of experience, muffling the sounds of the immediate environment and removing the individual from a synchronous community of listeners."[22] This is an ideal inter-personalization effect mirrored in experience. Much like silently reading a book, there is a one-to-one ratio between user and content, only with podcasting the listener doesn't have to guess what the creator sounds like. Their imagination and intellect must still be engaged in ways that aren't demanded by a visual medium (e.g., one must imagine the scenarios or stories being described in the podcast), but the listener also has the advantage of hearing the creator tell the story in the way that they wish for it to be told. For Lidgren, these sorts of effects have clear support from neuroscience as she cites Sillesen et al.'s 2015 meta-analysis of sixty psychological and neuroscientific studies that focuses on the potential impact of people's ability to feel empathy for characters in journalistic stories considering the recent cultural shift from print to digital formats. Sillesen et al. found that the literature supports the claim that the human brain is structured to empathically respond in interactions and that those responses increase as we learn more about each other. Additionally, the research supported the claim that "narratives spark feelings of empathy in much the same way, which is why stories have the power to influence minds and motivate action."[23] The reason for this is because we relate to others' pain and in doing so, "our brains intertwine our own and others' experiences."[24] For Lindgren, again speaking specifically of docu-feature podcasts like *This American Life* and *Serial*,

> This is relevant to understanding how personal storytelling is driving the current resurgence in radio and audio. By presenting stories that illustrate

> inner lives, the listener can relate them to his or her own experience and develop insight and understanding as they listen. . . . This type of intimate and personal storytelling sets up a platform where the audience can learn about themselves by hearing others grapple with emotional challenges.[25]

It hopefully should not seem like much of a leap to extrapolate the theoretical underpinnings of this research (which looks at journalistic content) and apply it to audio content that is fictional in nature. Certainly, one would think that poetry, given that it tends to be very personal and often non-fictive or confessional in nature, would be applicable to this sort of phenomena. However, the nonfictional narratives of docu-features are still narratives, especially since, as scholar Manuel Fernández-Sande points out that *This American Life* is "a classic example of narrative radio journalism. . . . A genre that applies the techniques of fiction to news production to give the settings, human subjects and topics addressed in a news story a heightened sense of drama, emotion or entertainment value that makes it more compelling to listeners."[26] This is to say that if the techniques of this sort of storytelling are the same or similar to those of fiction, one might imagine that fiction might create a similar effect. Indeed, much research has been done in this area, and it appears that the research does indeed bear this out.[27]

The technological possibilities of radio limited its use potentialities due to restrictions inherent to the medium itself. There were three major limitations. One, you had to be broadcasting to an area. Two, your audience had to live in that area and had to be listening when you were broadcasting. Three, your audience was limited by the strength of your transmitter, and strong transmitters were not cheap. This meant that only people with the capital and societal privilege to support these sorts of endeavors were able to pursue them, which then meant that these people became the gatekeepers of content for those mediums. All of these barriers expanded as they moved forward in time. The potentialities of podcasters of today seem limitless by comparison. The wonderful thing about today's podcasts is that they can be DIY and still be moderately successful compared to those that are backed by corporate interests if not more so. The only limitations on the creation of podcasts have to do with user acumen, which is hardly an issue considering the ease at which current software allows users to interact with their own voices.[28] This is because anyone with a phone or a laptop can make a podcast and distribute it on the internet. Also, the only barrier between the creator and their audience is visibility, which is to say creators have the option of finding their own audiences and promoting their own work to the specific communities to which they belong as opposed to being hired and promoted by a media conglomerate (many of whom have a vested interest in perpetuating a cultural narrative status quo). There are, of course, still systemic barriers that exist in these digital spaces as search engines and social media algorithms have been demonstrated to show racial and minority bias.[29] However, the proliferation of podcasts created by persons of minoritized groups is encouraging. This new lack of barriers to access is important for groups that had previously been barred from such large-scale audiences. Today's podcasts provide a platform for unlimited diversity in both content and audience.

Additionally, because of this medium's predilection for exponential expansion, a good deal of podcasts that address issues of craft as it pertains to creative writing already happen to exist (i.e., craft interview podcasts) and because the nature of podcasts embodies a diverse group of experiential perspectives. Creative writing instructors have these podcasts (just like everyone else does), which means we as writing instructors have the ability to introduce interviews with writers in a way that aligns with the diverse number of perspectives within our classrooms, which is something Leigh Camacho Rourks will be discussing in the next chapter.

2

The Many Voices Classroom*

Leigh Camacho Rourks

Like many creative writing professors who teach in minoritized communities, the issue of privileging traditional and dominant voices in the classroom (and in publishing) has been a concern over my entire career. However, working exclusively with students who have learning disabilities, ADHD, and autism spectrum disorders at Beacon College (a nonprofit liberal arts school dedicated to educating primarily neurodiverse students) has further crystalized my understanding of the role of the master/student dichotomy in fostering a homogenized writing and publishing community, which continues to silence marginalized voices. The desire to alter classroom power structures toward a more democratized learning environment is, of course, nothing new. However, as the writing world evolves, as new technologies emerge, as new fan bases grow, so can the tools we use in this fight. Podcasting is one such tool. Thanks to the abundance of podcasts by an ever-growing, rich, and diverse group of writers, creative writing teachers can create a many voices classroom. The "many voices" pedagogy focuses, with careful intentionality, on a variety

*Portions of this chapter first appeared in the March 2022 issue of the *Journal of Creative Writing Studies*, in our preliminary article on the subject, "The Virtues of Podcasting and Multimodal Literacies in the Creative Writing Classroom." They have since been revised and extended.

of diverse voices (including students' own) as teaching models, and it is a teaching ethos that specifically centers intersectionality.

One objective of this chapter is to explore the theoretical underpinnings and methodology for curating and utilizing podcasts to this end. In this way, professors expand student access to "living authors" beyond themselves, while empowering students to join a much larger discourse far beyond the limitations of their workshop and university. This chapter will also explore the ways using podcasts in a many voices class can help students learn how to better engage in this larger writing discourse themselves. Therefore, we will discuss how to utilize podcasts to model discourse, providing practical examples of assignments where students actively engage with the podcasts curated by their professor and even create their own podcasts in response.

Democratized Learning: From Sage on the Stage to Guide on the Side

American pedagogical philosophers and theorists have long focused on democratizing learning, often described as a move from traditional "sage on the stage" teaching methodologies to a "guide on the side" teaching mode. Current versions of the movement (revitalized across academia in the late twentieth century) lay in a desire to better reach a diverse set of students. For example, in 1993, the article "Every Course Differently: Diversity and College Teaching, An Outline," asks readers to envision a "metaphor of teaching more in line with theories of learning as construction . . . : coach, midwife, experienced companion (as opposed to the 'sage on the stage')."[1] At the core of this prodding lies the need to reach more students, not just those who look, think, and learn like the dominant homogeneity of teachers in higher education (which despite moves to diversify, still skews to a neurotypical white male). Nelson opens with the declaration:

> I believe that bias has been (and is) so deep in our society that no one is free of sexism, racism, and classism. Further, our ability to recognize bias is deepening rapidly so that having our teaching up to last year's standards usually leaves a lot for improvement this year.[2]

This is certainly still true, even in departments where discussion and workshop models dominate, and is why in "The Many Voices of the English Classroom," Turvey et al. argue that there is a "continuing need to conceptualize the English classroom as a social space where a number of voices meet."[3] These voices must extend past those few that are typical in academia, and in searching for them we must privilege diversity.

Although the creative writing workshop model was an early adopter of "guide on the side" principles in higher education, fully embracing the cooperative learning philosophies of early American pedagogy philosophers such as Parker and then Dewey, it is more often than not as competitive a learning model as any in American Higher Education, which tends toward Master/Student(s) power structures.[4] This is probably due to the necessarily performative nature of a model which can claim as its greatest proponents those who insist writing cannot be taught.[5] In this model, the professor is set as the class's "moderator" and "living example of an author," whom, it is assumed, the students will look to emulate.[6] As moderator, he may seem to be a "guide on the side," but as students' only example of a living author (especially in smaller programs), he is certainly their sage. The result ranges from students who parrot their professor to those who vie so hard for dominance in his eyes as to make the workshop a hazing experience and, as McGurl explains, "an occasion for violence done to the youthful writer."[7]

Both of these problems can be brutally amplified for minoritized students. In *The Anti-Racist Writing Workshop*, Felicia Rose Chavez tells of being asked to work closely with a professor who she dislikes, who belittles her, who wants from her something very different than what she wants for herself.[8] Despite this, she agrees because, she explains, "How could I say no? Here was a professor of color, investing his time and energy in me, my future, an advantage he played weekly: 'What you fail to understand, Felicia, is the magnitude of my gesture.'"[9] Despite her dislike, despite his condescension, despite the inner voice that told her not to work with him, faced with this "sage," she pushes herself to quiet her own voice: "Use his words, I told myself. Sound like him so that he hears you. Do not fail to understand. Do not fail."[10] The pressure for all students is certainly great, but for those that see few faces like their own, the pressure to please a mentor, to not fail, can be crippling. The bullying can come from anywhere, even those "sages" who believe, perhaps too much, that (through "gestures of great magnitude") they are helping those same students.

The core issue returns us to Nelson's concerns vis-à-vis bias. Despite extensive discussion of its flaws among teaching, writing, and publishing professionals, the workshop model is still at the heart of most creative writing classes and programs. Unfortunately, it requires a certain homogeneity that can discourage diversity of thought. It can especially leave minority and disadvantaged students at best silenced, at worst attacked. This is an issue that prevails despite our knowledge and discussion of its presence and damage. In Junot Díaz's famous *New Yorker* article, "MFA *vs.* POC," he quickly gets to the heart of the issue: "So what was the problem? Oh just the standard problem of MFA programs. That shit was too white," he says of his own workshop experience.[11] He goes on, "Too white as in my workshop reproduced exactly the dominant culture's blind spots and assumptions around race and racism (and sexism and heteronormativity, etc.)."[12] What is ironic is Díaz's own documented predatory sexism in the classrooms; though with hindsight, the fact that sexism and heteronormativity appear as a parenthetical, an afterthought, seems an early clue to Díaz's now (horribly) clear biases.

Nelson's warning that it is not enough to discuss bias (and beyond that, violence) feels especially prescient in this case. In "Unsilencing the Writing Workshop," Beth Nguyen discusses the ways the traditional workshop model silences BIPOC. She tells the story of having to stay silent in workshop as her white classmates discuss what dim sum is (instead of her story), not only wasting her time but colonizing the concept of "common knowledge."[13] As a doctoral student, I submitted a piece of flash fiction titled "Pulpo" to our fiction workshop, and sat and listened while the class argued over whether I needed to define the term "pulpo" (which in Spanish means octopus) for readers. What amazed me was the number of my friends, sitting in my workshop, who didn't bother to look the word up before our class, instead using our short time for an argument which never needed to happen. Jimin Han tells of how she struggles to get any feedback at all from some members of her workshop: "I've been in workshops where my classmates and the teacher either prescribed a path for me to write a story or novel with which they were comfortable, not knowing what I was trying to accomplish, or saying nothing because they felt they didn't understand my life experience enough to comment."[14] In his Code Switch article, "When Defending Your Writing Becomes Defending Yourself," Matthew Salesses collected many similar stories; among them was this one:

> Writer Jackson Bliss describes an experience when a Pakistani writer spoke up in defense of a Desi character Bliss had written, and "the workshop rejected his comments and then spoke over him. Think about that for a second," Bliss writes, "a group of mostly white writers telling a hapa writer and a Pakistani writer what was culturally authentic and culturally permissible . . . about nonwhite people."[15]

There should be nothing surprising about these experiences. Similar experiences have been documented repeatedly and repeatedly and repeatedly by minoritized writers. Many of us have witnessed or experienced this firsthand. And yet it still happens.

Tragically, we tend to play down the long-term damage this does to both the careers of these writers and to the writers themselves. Chavez explains in *The Anti-Racist Writing Workshop*: the traditional "silencing" in workshop "particularly for writers of color, is especially destructive in institutions that routinely disregard the lived experiences of people who are not white. This matrix of silence is so profound it enlists writers of color to eradicate ourselves."[16] Ignoring this profound problem is not an option. Nor is pretending bias clouds everyone but ourselves. Our biases and privileges are often subconscious, hard to see, much less acknowledge even to ourselves. Therefore, our teaching practices must be, as Nelson suggested, not just checked and rechecked but changed and changed again. The alternative can have devastating results we may never see, but those who receive the wounds will not soon forget them.

The Many Voices Classroom and the Podcast

Considering that the Pew Research Center has found 76 percent of college and university faculty (and 81 percent of full professors) are white, the homogeneous workshop is a reflection of the homogeneous faculty system.[17] In this system, the workshop is a force of erasure of marginalized identities because the workshop is a place where the author's silence is mandated, encouraged, or, in some cases, simply safer. When the author is the only BIPOC in the room (or one of the only), their experience is minoritized to the point of full erasure, especially when the classroom's "sage" is the blueprint for the class's homogeneity. One way to avoid this sort of closed system is for the creative writing classroom to expand into a many voices model. The many voices pedagogy is most closely aligned with social justice teaching, and at its core is an ethos of diversity. For example, the Many Voices Reading Group studied by Julie Botticello was "set up to counter dominant narratives and white knowledge bases underpinning higher education systems" and "the readings for Many Voices were selected to offer academic mentors who have created legacies of empowerment in their writing, so that students could follow their example in their works."[18] The key to serving a diverse group of student writers is to provide a large and diverse community for them to learn from.

Many of us work hard to create classes dedicated to diversity, and we provide readings from a variety of authors. But it can be difficult to achieve a many voices course from readings alone. Balancing student reading loads (especially in a workshop class where reading loads are already quite high) is a challenge we all face. Additionally, frequently updating those reading lists in order to constantly battle the ways in which our own biases affect our decisions creates a dramatic rise in teacher workload. Moreover, studies have shown that university students read astonishingly little of what is assigned to them before class. For example, studies showed reading compliance of psychology students at all levels to be below 30 percent and there is evidence that this low level of compliance is fairly standard in all majors—even English majors.[19] Finally, even those students who dig in and read every single assignment are not in fact "hearing" the voice behind those readings. Reading is a single modality, but research shows the necessity for incorporating multiple modalities in the classroom, engaging "multiliteracies [which set] out to stretch literacy beyond the constraints of official standard forms of written and spoken language to connect with the culturally and linguistically diverse landscapes."[20] This need is highlighted in writing classes with multilingual and neurodivergent learners, whose needs are generally overlooked in standard creative writing classes despite the fact that both groups are prevalent in all our universities.

Therefore, to truly create a many voices classroom, other modalities must be considered.

The diversity of voices found in podcasts today makes centering an intersectional ethos fairly straight forward. Changing out podcasts each semester, thus inviting new voices and new discussions into the classroom is not difficult, as prep time becomes minimal. Additionally, as they can be listened to in class, compliance can be raised drastically to all students who attend the session. In my experience, even when assigned as homework, students appear to comply at a much greater rate. The general popularity of podcasts means many of my students are already fans of the medium. And those who are not are often excited to have a new way to engage. However, perusal of the literature, scholarly and popular, indicates a widespread unease with the idea of audio materials replacing traditional visual reading. As Have and Pederson point out, the medium of a story is important and the move between mediums is "not frictionless . . . . A story changes when it is moved to another medium, and strategies of analysis must therefore be developed which are sensitive to these material and technological differences."[21] This is not a weakness but a strength. Listening to authors read and discuss work does not replace assigned readings but provides a different modality which encourages students to exercise new analytical pathways. Ultimately, when considering assigning texts, the definition of "reading should not be reduced to the visual decoding of writing but can also be an auditive decoding of an audiobook, which offers a different form of literary experience."[22] Podcasts change this dynamic further, because they focus on active and immediate discourse—lively discussion. The writing community comes alive in podcasts, and students have a chance to experience living voices in concert, and the opportunities to amplify minoritized voices are magnified. Additionally, when assigned outside of the classroom, they also provide many benefits associated with increasing student autonomy, retention, and learning. Research has shown that not only do podcasts provide students with "flexibility and convenience," "the ability to catch up on content," and "the capability of reducing distance-student isolation" (an issue whose importance has become increasingly clear throughout the Covid pandemic and which we know will continue to be necessary to consider throughout the future) but they also foster greater "student engagement" and are responsible for "improving learning and boosting the learning experience."[23]

It is certainly true that podcasts are not a magic bullet. Used without care, they can act as a barrier for students with auditory disabilities, auditory processing disorders, attention deficit disorders, and other disabilities. It is important to note that no matter what visual or auditory media a professor utilizes in class, it must be accompanied with standard accommodations such as pausing regularly for processing delay and attention loss, providing transcripts when available and outlines when they are not (though programs such as otter.ai make creating transcripts fairly easy when none are available), and offering options for re-watching/listening outside of the classroom. Sustained watching or listening can be difficult for many people. Among the many forms of diversity we must all consider is the diversity of disability. Not all students self-identify for accommodations for a variety of complex reasons (such as avoiding stigma, difficulty in maneuvering the steps necessary to receive accommodation, and universities' general unfamiliarity with certain disabilities); therefore, providing blanket accommodations such as these can improve the quality of education for everyone. In fact, these accommodations benefit a wide variety of students, including those less familiar with the subject area or whose cultural discourse is markedly different from either academic discourse or that which is specific to the field of creative writing. Accommodations help everyone, especially in this case.

Modeling Agreement, Modeling Dissent: Podcasts Model Dialogue

Professors who curate podcasts that provide a broad range of viewpoints on the life and craft of writing, even those they disagree with, have a unique opportunity rarely found outside of team teaching—modeling vibrant academic discourse. In the team-teaching model, students "see that it [is] possible to disagree about fundamental issues and still respect the integrity of your opponent without being hostile" (Anderson and Speck). Considering how hostile workshops have been historically, this modeling seems paramount to the success of making the creative writing classroom better able to serve our students, especially those most often harmed in workshop.

I may not have considered how strong a need there is for additional "teachers" in our creative writing classrooms if I'd not recently had the opportunity to team teach a Humanities course with a professor from a different field. We both attended and participated in every class during the semester. We often viewed materials through quite different (and at times opposing) lenses, and we did not hide that from our students. We modeled learning from each other, through disagreement and dialogue. Student engagement was very high, with students delighted by our differences, often laughing with *and* at us, and intellectually challenging us more than I have experienced in traditional class environments. What we modeled, they embraced. In *Team Teaching: What, Why, and How?* Francis Buckley explains that "The clash of teacher viewpoints, changes of voice and rhythm, and alternation of different styles and personalities are stimulating and exciting. This gets and keeps attention and prevents boredom."[24] It would seem that our experience is replicated across curriculums. Unfortunately, in most American universities, team teaching continues to be a rare opportunity that most teachers and students will never experience.

Luckily, some of its most important benefits can translate to a classroom in which the teacher curates and shares podcasts utilizing the many voices ethos. Francis Buckley provides an extended list of ways team teaching can help students:

- Team teaching can also offset the danger of imposing ideas, values, and mind-sets on minorities or less powerful ethnic groups. Teachers of different backgrounds can culturally enrich one another and the students.
- In this context, both students and teachers learn. Listening skills grow. Knowledge is related to life. Schooling is transformed into lifelong learning.
- With so many opportunities to compare techniques, students learn to evaluate themselves, other students, and teachers more accurately.[25]

These three benefits are especially germane to the problems with traditional creative writing instruction. The reason why team teaching is so powerful is its ability to center diversity in voice and thought as "normal." This normalization of difference is missing across academia, and creative writing workshops are a microcosm of that bigger issue. Fortunately, podcasts center writers instead of centering academia. They are specifically meant for lay people and professionals looking for input outside of classrooms. With classrooms being so homogeneous, this is exactly why we need them.

It is true that students' main model of discourse is generally also external to academia. However, what they tend to learn as "normal" lacks the same element of difference as we see in the "ivory tower." For a large number of our students normal discourse growing up excludes those outside of their own social networks (whether virtual or the "real life" ones in their schools, churches, neighborhoods, and parental friend groups) and is dominated by their own race, ethnicity, sexuality, class, political leanings, and other identity groupings. It is no wonder that workshop can result in micro-aggressions, digging insults, and even violent, hostile discussion, as most students' main model of discourse is shared between both non-academic, homogenous discourses and discourses which are solely for entertainment purposes. The popularity of violent and demeaning discourse as entertainment is no secret and highlights exactly how problematic students' beginning models are. They are entrenched and particularly difficult to escape.

However, professors do influence students by modeling linguistic behavior. The limitations on any single professor here are, unfortunately, obvious. In order to change the linguistic modality, it is probably not enough to simply listen to podcasts in classes. Instead, a professor must engage actively and encourage their students to do so as well. It is similar to teaching students active reading, where we model the discourse of annotation for students. With podcasts, a professor can put one on for the class, pause it regularly to engage, to talk back, to agree and disagree, to muse, to comment. They can (and should) even open up the dialogue to students in real time. This achieves much the same sort of modeling as team teaching. In my own class, after pausing podcasts a couple of times to consider the topic further or even disagree with the speaker, my students have started calling out "pause!" or "wait, wait!"

when they hear something they want to discuss further (or "clap back at"). They come to enjoy this so much that they are critiquing whole programs by the end of the semester. Recently, the class decided to dissect and reject the host's choice of interim music on a podcast; luckily this was right before they created their own, so not only was it (spontaneously) on topic but it was also very helpful. Students can be keen "readers" of audio texts and they can learn to find their own authority when given a chance. Even better, students who are encouraged to talk back (and forth) to these podcasts (with the help of teacher modeling) begin to feel part of the larger discourse in a very literal and practical way. With appropriately curated podcasts, this ultimately entrenches the idea that diversity of approach and thought positively enhances our world and our writing.

Practical Application: Curating Podcasts for the Classroom

Perhaps one of the most difficult things about curating podcasts to share with students is becoming a part of the listening community yourself. However, it is a joyous problem to have. I would suggest against searching "creative writing" on your favorite podcasting app. When I started listening to creative writing podcasts, I almost gave up because the sheer abundance was intimidating. What works better is to talk to your colleagues and friends. Most are more than happy to share their favorite writing podcast or, more often than not, tell you about the one they were recently invited to speak on or the one they themselves have started.

I also find engaging students in the task of choosing podcast episodes can really increase engagement. I often make a list of podcasts and ask each student to choose a particular episode and come to class and make an argument that the episode they have chosen is the one we should listen to together. This serves quite a few goals. It places the onus of our class material partially in student hands which I find increases students' feelings of community and personal stakes in the class, it also encourages students to "sample" quite a few episodes (and maybe even get hooked!), and finally, I have found that it fosters a more healthy source of competition than the workshop ever would, and it seems many students love to compete and will find a way to do it, one way or another. It also helps me prep, which is great.

Sample Assignments to Accompany Listening to Podcasts

Class Journal: Podcast Response (low-level creative writing courses)

For questions 2–4, write roughly a paragraph.

(1) Title of Podcast, Episode, and Speakers/Authors

(2) Why do you think we listened to this podcast and what did you gain from it as a writer (if you answer that you gained nothing, you will get a zero on this assignment, so consider carefully)?

(3) What was the most valuable moment in this piece (for informative pieces and interviews) or interesting use of imagery or sound (for creative pieces) and why?

(4) If this piece had characters, who was your favorite or least favorite and why (if not, skip this)?

Comments: This assignment is designed as low risk/high reward and is designed to foster engagement and prime class discussion

Class Journal: Reading and Podcast Response (all other creative writing courses)

Write a letter in response to today's reading or podcast, addressed to the author of the work or the author being interviewed.

(1) In addressing your letter, make sure to spell your author's name correctly and to use all appropriate honorifics.

(2) Utilize the body of the letter to discuss what you learned from the author and how you might apply that to your own work or writing life.

(3) Discuss how the writer's approach or work or philosophy may or may not be different from your own and how both those similarities and differences are learning opportunities for you as a writer and a member of the writing community.

(4) Consider what questions you might have for the author.

(5) Thank the author for their time.

Comments: Though I do not ask or require students to send these letters, some do. Whether or not they do, an assignment like this asks the student to see themselves as a part of the larger writing community and imagine themselves as a valid member of the greater conversation.

3

Craft and Metacognition[*]

Leigh Camacho Rourks

Re-Envisioning the Reading and Writing Self: A Metacognitive Approach to Learning Craft

In order to truly be a part of the many voices classroom discussed in Chapter 2, students must find their own voices, find confidence in those voices, and find value in their classmates' voices. As the many voices model holds at its center an ethos of shared experience from a variety of diverse personal lenses, it is imperative that student voice be just as centered as the voices of "experts." Podcasting is a wonderful route to achieve this. In a class where the professor has modeled ongoing craft discussion through podcasts curated to fill the course with a wealth of craft views, the next step is to ask the learners to engage craft in much the same way, directly in a podcast. By doing so, instructors encourage students to learn as much about their own voice, their own knowledge, their own processes as they have learned about those of others. The rewards of this sort of knowledge extend far beyond creative writing.

The fact that podcasting provides learners with a multimodal experience is one of its greatest strengths. Encouraging student writers to consider and

---

[*]Portions of this chapter first appeared in the March 2022 issue of the *Journal of Creative Writing Studies*, in our preliminary article on the subject, "The Virtues of Podcasting and Multimodal Literacies in the Creative Writing Classroom." They have since been revised and extended.

compose texts through multimodality is nothing new. According to *Remixing Composition: A History of Multimodal Writing Pedagogy*, since the 1960s, compositionists have been working on similar goals as we are to "articulate the interconnections among alphabetic writings, speaking, reading, and listening"; "demonstrate the ways that auditory forms of composing can enhance the invention and revision of alphabetic texts"; and "question the hegemony of print writing and composition, arguing for the importance of valuing auditory forms of knowing."[1] For example, Peter Elbow's focus on teaching students to read their writing aloud, as they compose—"If we read out loud each sentence we've written and keep revising or fiddling with it till it sounds right—till every part fits comfortably in the mouth and sounds right in the ear—the meaning will be clear and often forceful"[2]—was a call for a multimodal approach to writing instruction, one that explicitly hinged on voice. This focus on voice as both a literal aural production and what Elbow saw as resonance[3] (another—quite purposeful—metaphor hinging on the embodied voice) provides a gap that creative writing students can fill through aural texts.

Elbow points out that resonate voice in writing is more powerful than speech because, unlike speech, writing "has always served as a crucial place for trying out parts of the self or unconscious that have been hidden or neglected or underdeveloped—to experiment."[4] It is important then to consider how what our students do in a podcast can be very different than normal "speech." Podcasting is, even when unscripted, a performative, creative, and textual act, which lends itself to the same sorts of trial and experimentation for which Elbow praised writing. Unscripted podcasts tend to have at minimum loose outlines that value research, pre-planning, and are consciously focused on audience. The parameters a teacher gives in an assignment can lean more heavily on one or all of these, by requiring a more formal outline or even script, for example. Ultimately podcasts, even those whose charm hinges on spontaneity, are at their core made things (the Greek *poíēma* "the made thing" or poem, comes to mind), much closer to alphabetic writing than most other aural engagements. Therefore, student podcasts can reveal a resonant voice, like their writing, that is all their own. In fact, it may be easier to find or examine one's voice in this mode since the podcast lies somewhere between writing (whether it is scripted or loosely outlined) and spontaneous everyday speech. This means the podcast is uniquely suited to helping students share and consider their own voice, both literally and figuratively.

Unfortunately, "voice" is one of those craft terms that so many of us struggle to define, not just for our students but even for ourselves. It is a messy business. Our language for the discussion of voice is almost entirely metaphoric and the term itself is used for no singular measurable item and instead for a collection of nebulous ideas. One of the most difficult issues to parse when teaching voice is the way it is undeniably linked to identity, despite the fact that a writer's voice on the page may not mimic their literal, aural-voice, but instead represent the voice of a persona or even a dramatic voice. This dilemma in discussions of voice (identity *vs.* persona *vs.* performance) holds true in a podcast as much as it does on the page. In creating a podcast, students have near-complete control over the end product (unlike in class discussion or in the typical presentation format of standing in front of the class to speak). As with traditional creative writing work, students can plan ahead as much or as little as they like. They can re-record, edit, cut, and manipulate the language in the same ways as writing (even as the methodologies differ—though with "cut" and "paste" existing in both word processors and digital audio workstations, editing audio and editing text are not as different as one might imagine). Additionally, manipulating the physical sound of their biologic, aural-voice is as simple as experimenting with software (which can change pitch, timber, speed, and much, much more) or even physical, real-world effects (such as standing in a bathtub or a field when recording). Finally, students can create a dramatic voice by having someone else speak for them, and read their work and ideas from a script (this option is both necessary artistically and as an accommodation for an array of disabilities). With so many ways to augment or even mask the author's original aural-voice, the quandary of voice becomes a particularly interesting one for students to consider in their own podcasts. It requires an extremely recursive examination of their textual products, their aural products, and their own preconceived notions (or lack thereof) on the concept of voice and its position in discussions of craft. In such introspection, metacognitive learning is awakened.

Metacognitive learning "includes two components: a) our knowledge of concepts, ourselves, the task at hand and strategies we are using (metacognitive knowledge); b) planning and setting goals, monitoring, and evaluating our performance and learning (metacognitive regulation)."[5] Metacognitive learning exercises require students to do a deep dive into their own knowledge and understanding. They have been shown to have long-lasting positive results. For example, metacognition "has been linked to . . . successful transfer of writing skills across the curriculum,"[6] is "a common trait among successful professionals,"[7] and produces "high-level cognitive functions such as reasoning, critical thinking and problem-solving."[8] Building metacognitive knowledge and regulation in creative writing courses may seem especially (or even, only) important to those teaching lower-level creative writing courses and those courses that function as a piece of a more general liberal arts education, where students may or may not see creative writing in their future but who, we all know, can gain much from exploring the art. However, even at a graduate level, metacognition is an important component to success, in writing and in every other part of their current studies and future work. According to Mitsea and Drigas, "the implementation of metacognitive strategies empowers higher-order cognitive abilities, attentional and memory control, self-confidence and leads to independent and meaningful learning."[9] Regardless of level, all of our students gain when we incorporate metacognitive assignments, and podcasting is an excellent way to foster these cognitive gains.

The ways podcasts enrich learning innately overlap with the strengths of metacognition, as they give learners power over their own education and in doing so encourage thinking about not just what they learn, but also how they learn. When listening to podcasts outside of the classroom, students control many aspects of their education, the environment, timing, pace, and so on. This enhances metacognitive regulation and encourages self-awareness (or reflexive thinking). In producing podcasts, students have even greater control. Nelson, Anderson, and Dau's literature review for their conference paper *Podcasts as a Learning Media in Higher Education* found that standing research and later their own backs this up: "podcasts supports [*sic*] active, social and creative aspects of learning and strengthen reflection and self-regulated learning."[10] Podcasts require multimodal interaction and produce dynamic and recursive thinking.

The Voice of Exploration: Speaking Our Truths, Revising Our Understandings

In my classroom, students make podcasts as a metacognitive exercise in exploration of their own ideas and theories of craft. Both metacognitive knowledge and metacognitive regulation are at the heart of craft discussions and revision (the reflexivity needed to consider craft and revision is also the core element of metacognitive thinking, after all). This means that craft discussions and revision activities are particularly suited for the implementation of purposeful, strategic metacognitive learning strategies. As we have seen, doing so (especially when the "different facets [knowledge and regulation] of metacognition are optimized") improves not only immediate learning but also student's longer-term performance.[11] When paired with revision portfolios, students' pointed and planned discussions of their own work, voice, and process pushes them to explore their declarative, procedural, and conditional knowledge about writing.

One way I achieve this is by having students interview each other after having completed revision portfolios (in some cases, students interview themselves or I interview them). The podcast interview is an emerging writing form that hinges on prepared questions based on the interviewee's work, requiring students to engage deeply both as readers and as writers, testing and growing their own understanding of craft through partnership, then refining it as they find ways to articulate their ideas for a larger audience (either of their fellow students, when played to the class as a whole, or in the greater world, if the podcasts are published). The project pushes students to consciously form craft discussions as a genre with a clear, established audience (even in replaying the podcast to themselves the act of negotiation between writer and audience is acutely obvious, as the sound of their voice moves outside their heads—a separate entity, almost).

In classes where students have already been exposed to similar podcasts by established writers, it becomes easy to encourage them to see their own work, and their own thinking about their work (metacognition), as a part of a larger conversation within the literary community. This level of introspection allows "students to learn to take control of their own learning by defining goals, and monitoring their progress in achieving them,"[12] and because it is done in service of a larger discussion, they begin to orient their goals and progress within the more diverse literary community (or more diverse than we often find in our classrooms). This is especially helpful for first-generation college students and students whose backgrounds are underrepresented in the workshop. These students tend to feel like outsiders and are in danger of having their voices devalued by their peers in very homogeneous creative writing classes. Or, like me, they may squelch their own voice and identity to better fit into a perhaps unstated but clear definition of "literary" writing fostered in traditional workshop. Despite the fact that I am a Cuban-American woman whose identity is tied deeply to the Gulf South, the stories that I produced in my undergraduate workshops grew to be about placeless men, devoid of accent or voice. I moved from funny, almost surreal, stories of southern women attempting to survive their world to Hemingwayesque stories which seemed more appropriate to literary writing. I didn't even realize I had stripped so much of my voice out of my writing until much, much later. My experience is not unique and was far less traumatic than those of many other students. When this happens, students are robbed of their authoritative voice and learn to devalue risk. In *Podcasting and Performativity: Multimodal Invention in an Advanced Writing Class*, Leigh A. Jones found that podcasting (in this case, before writing) helped students build confidence in their own authority, take more risks in their writing, and become comfortable with their authorial voice.[13]

This is especially important considering the ways the term "craft" is encoded with ethnic, racial, and social bias, often with no clear recognition that perceptions of aesthetics and narrative structure are culturally defined. There is a wealth of research on this in both Linguistic and ESL/EFL studies. However, a deep scan of our workshops can show us these embedded cultural differences at play (or it can if we are lucky to have diverse classrooms and are open to the idea that what we have learned about craft may not be entirely true). In *Pleiades*' series "'Pure Craft' Is a Lie" (which later became part of the book *Craft in the Real World*), Matthew Salesses looks at the implications of these differences when they are met with traditional craft discussions. He opens the series by establishing the problem: "we base 'craft' off of what affects a literary, American reader. But that reader has already grown up with a world in which meaning is constructed in a certain way."[14] The implication is that we risk silencing voices when we invoke craft with a sense of reverence and purity. There is, then, much to be gained by asking students what they think of craft. An easy way to prime the pump for true introspection is to introduce the class to Salesses's essays first. In this way, students can be introduced (again and in new ways) to the importance of frank discourse in our field. It energizes their own search for their foundational beliefs about writing and loosens the tongues of students who might otherwise feel disinclined to disagree out loud, where it can be dangerous, especially for the minoritized.

I saw the power podcasting has in granting students authority and encouraging them to take it and grow in confidence firsthand in a recent class. I gave students a list of topics to explore in their podcasts, told them they had to include a one-page reading of their work, and showed them how to use an easy, free podcasting app (Anchor). Then, as an experiment, I let them go with no further parameters; while I suggested the podcasts span a time of ten minutes or so per person, I gave no hard and fast rule on length. Because my class was very small (six students) and is a non-majors introductory course, I felt comfortable providing them with more freedom than usual. Two of my students turned in a delightful hour and a half discussion on writing. A listener would probably not realize that these were anthrozoology and psychology majors that had no real desire to be writers in the long term. They could not stop talking about their writing, their ideas on writing, other people's writing, what they didn't understand about writing, and what they believed about the craft. They showed such confidence not only about what they believed they knew but also when discussing what they didn't know. It was a glorious listen, if long.

Then there is X, a student who is a graphic artist with a passion for writing, and who has the potential for a career as a writer if she so chooses. She is quiet and a bit of a loner. She is African American. She (like many of my students) has a learning disability. She has a vision for her creative work that is not part of the traditional homogeneity found in most workshops. She chose to interview herself for this project, and in doing so she blossomed. I was allowed to see a side of her I had not yet experienced in class. She spoke with authority and conviction, returning to many of our class discussions, often in order to upend them with questions and critique. She also explored her own relationship with writing and her process. She was particularly pensive about her own reluctance to revise her portfolio work, despite her belief in revision's importance. In interviewing herself, she chose risky questions, pushed herself past easy answers. She utilized the assignment to be creative, not only in exploring herself but also in pushing the genre of the podcast interview. Through her unrelenting performance of internal dialogue, she ultimately provided a clear path to additional revisions she believed her work needed and a discussion of how it had changed thus far.

Not only did X and the others successfully explore craft in their podcasts, they each had engaged in productive metacognitive explorations and the level of introspection that can "enhance learners' academic achievement, self-confidence and raise self-awareness."[15] In their podcasts, they achieved a deeper level of craft discussion (and productive disagreement, whether with each other or with ideas the class as a whole had discussed) than I had seen all semester. The freedoms I gave them placed the burden of autonomy on the students themselves, and by doing so seemed to increase their authoritative voice. Maybe of more profound importance to a writing classroom is the metacognitive exercise's illuminative properties:

> Imagine metacognition like a tunnel (such as a tunnel of time) and metacognitive strategies like the vehicle which could unveil countless and possible paths with the same destination: the stream of consciousness. This stream of luminosity becomes gradually visible as people make a journey in new, alternative or more trodden paths and climb the ladder of knowledge, bridging information gaps in a meaningful whole.[16]

This illumination is an excellent path to voice, and in creating their own metacognitive podcasts exploring craft, students are allowed to explore it.

Practical Application: Metacognitive Podcasting Assignments and Advice

There are many ways to assign metacognitive podcasts. In crafting any metacognitive assignment there are different goals which you can forefront. For example, a metacognitive exercise focusing on metacognitive regulation that is done after writing (or even after revision) may forefront self-assessment, but one done before writing begins may forefront planning or monitoring. Though in truth, metacognitive strategies are delineated and defined in a variety of ways by different researchers, Oualid Nemouchi lists ten categories that are embraced in most of the literature:

(1) Planning
(2) Monitoring
(3) Evaluating
(4) The Knowledge Monitoring Skill
(5) Cooperative Learning
(6) Self-Reflection and Management
(7) Metacognitive Scaffolding
(8) Modeling
(9) Self-Questioning
(10) Thinking Aloud and Self-Explanation[17]

Podcasting is well suited to serve any and all of these categories, so podcasting assignments are rich with possibilities.

Leigh A. Jones suggests opening the semester with podcasting, before official writing assignments are completed, and though her focus is on academic writing and not creative writing, her reasoning is sound in either field. Jones found that students were more comfortable exploring their ideas and taking risks orally than in alphabetic text, thus providing a sturdy platform for growth of an authoritative voice unafraid of risk in their school writing.[18] Additionally, she found by sharing podcasts early in the semester, her students built a strong community: "Students became familiar and comfortable with each other early on, and this comfort manifested itself in more engaged writing groups in which students became invested in each other's progress and success over the course of the semester."[19] Students used these podcasts for planning future work, and in doing so engaged their cohort in their future work, creating healthy stakes for workshopping groups.

I tend to pair my podcasts with the Midterm and Final, allowing students to monitor their knowledge and regulatory growth over the semester. I pair these with portfolio revisions, so that students focus on their application of craft and the way they are building their own scaffolded understanding of craft that may even clash with mine (the podcasts I share early on foster a comfort with clashing ideas as a part of good academic dialogue). However, I have found that I am not always capable of building this into the schedule (or keeping it). For example, as covid changed the way our classes were taught and changed our overall schedule, I found sparing class time to guide students in how to create a podcast, even with the most simple software, and providing students in class time to meet with partners and plan (especially over video conferencing) difficult. I was not, however, willing to forgo the benefits of our podcasting completely. In this case, I interviewed students for a class podcast at the end of the semester. I provided the class with the questions I would ask beforehand and warned them I would also throw in some spontaneous questions based on their individual work. Then I recorded our session and edited it on my own. In this case our podcast was my gift to the students at the end of the semester. They can listen later and hear their own voices, their own authorial authority and reconnect to our class once again. Still, when at all possible, I think it best to put students in charge of their own podcasts, and by extension their own voices. As Jones found, "Recording the podcast in solitude or with one partner also gave students more time and the creative autonomy to construct an authoritative persona." Unfortunately, when I recorded our podcast, not only was I unable to give students as much autonomy over the sound but they also really did lack that time element (perhaps the most scarce resource in our classes) Jones is referring to.

One thing that is an absolute necessity in creating podcasting exercises is a modicum of flexibility on the instructor's part. Not only do flexible assignments open the door to student autonomy and creative risk-taking but any assignment so heavily reliant on software can also meet with unforeseen problems. Luckily, podcasts can be made in person or across space and time. They can use advanced methods on the computer or simple cell phone apps. It is, inherently, a flexible genre; nonetheless, issues do arise. One summer I had a student who could not find a partner and couldn't imagine interviewing herself, so I had her write out the questions, and I interviewed her. I have had students terrified of learning even simple new programs, students with paralyzing fear of public speaking, and students with auditory processing disorders for whom creating a podcast was at its core an unfair assignment due to their learning differences. By allowing students a variety of options (such as working alone or in groups, individual help in recording, having an "actor" perform the student's part, or even, in the case of students with aural/oral disabilities offering another multimodal genre to work in), instructors can foresee and dodge many difficulties.

Metacognitive Podcasting Sample Assignment

Podcast Assignment: Who are you, the writer? Who do you want to be?
This assignment can be done as pairs or on your own.

- Purpose: This metacognitive assignment should help you reflect on your own writing process, quirks, goals, difficulties, and strengths BUT it is also designed to help you create a creative nonfiction piece which uses your creativity to help listeners a peek into your writing and reading mind
- Options:
  - Two class members interview each other (this option should run roughly twice as long as the others: 20–30 minutes)
  - A class member has an outside person interview them with questions the student wrote (10–15 minutes)
  - A single class member tells a story of their writing and reading journey (10–15 minutes)
    - For this option, you may also write this as a script and have another student perform the voice recording (acting as your "voice")
- Requirements
  - You will read one piece or excerpt a piece you are proud of writing and revising during our time in this class (3–5 minutes)

- You will discuss
  - What qualities *you* enjoy in the literature you read (beyond genre—think of craft elements we have been studying, for example)
    - Give at least two specific examples from works you enjoy reading, at least one of which must have been read for this class (read very short excerpts and describe what they are doing that you enjoyed from our class readings or one of your classmate's shared work)
    - Discuss at least three of the following
      - Your influences
      - Your goals
      - Your writing practice
      - Your writing style
      - Your writing strengths
      - Your writing difficulties
      - Your writing desires
      - Your writing quirks or rituals
- Plan and record your podcast (remember you can do as many "takes" as you want and can edit out mistakes if you choose)
  - Possible podcast software: Audacity (for computer), Anchor (cell phone)
  - We will have a tutorial in class and you can find a series of tutorials in the resources folder
- Extra Credit will be given to students who incorporate sound in ways which enhance the podcast (see resources folder and class notes)
- We will listen to all podcasts as a class

4

Fiction

Multimodality and the Storytelling Podcast[*]

Saul Lemerond

Oral storytelling is arguably the oldest known medium. Storytelling exists in all cultures, and its value depends upon the story's ability to communicate knowledge that can be abstracted and applied to a potentiality of situations. As Greenfield and Lave put it, storytelling presupposes the "ability to generalize from the familiar [problem-solving situations] to unfamiliar problem-solving situations."[1] This is to say that human beings have always used stories to inform their listeners whether it be concrete or abstract, or maybe more accurately, directly instructional, informally recreational, or some combination of those, depending on the goals of the storyteller.[2] This chapter will discuss benefits that the fictional, narrative storytelling podcast can have for students (and for their understanding of themselves as creators) and argue for podcast's

[*]Portions of this chapter first appeared in the March 2022 issue of the *Journal of Creative Writing Studies*, in our preliminary article on the subject, "The Virtues of Podcasting and Multimodal Literacies in the Creative Writing Classroom." They have since been revised and extended.

inclusion by pointing to the inherent benefits to student's learning and self-understanding as they are challenged to write, cast, direct, and create their stories in podcast form. This while, and I don't think this can be understated, at the same time providing them with applicable, practical knowledge in a digital space that continues to flourish. As has been mentioned, and at the time of this book's release, there are millions of podcasts and hundreds of millions of podcast listeners. More people are creating content for potential mass audiences than ever before, and more money is being invested in podcasts, whether it be through small individual fees or donations or by large hosting sites like Stitcher or Spotify (or even multimedia streaming services like Netflix) paying for exclusive rights to some individual podcasting content. This is a resurgence of audio mediums on a massive scale. A vast diversity of creative spaces are presenting themselves. And this means individual creators, or more importantly, individual storytellers, have an opportunity for their stories to reach larger audiences than previously thought possible. This is to say that creators, where it may have previously been impossible for them to discover a significant audience for themselves, now have the potential to reach much larger audiences than ever before with much less effort, and with far fewer barriers to access. For instance, where in the past amateur creators could often only expect their close friends and family members to engage with their content, now social media, message boards, and hosting sites have made it possible for creators to discover like-minded communities eager to engage.

Metacognitive and Multimodal Frameworks: Represented within and as Self

There is a clear pedagogical framework that speaks to the value in challenging students to not only study storytelling podcasts but also create them. That said, I will begin by giving a brief summary of multimodality and metacognition as a reciprocal pedagogical model. When I say multimodal, I use the definition of modes, and the list of those modalities, as outlined by the New London School: written language, oral language, visual representation, gestural representation, spatial representation, tactile representation, and most importantly, the representation of the self. The idea is that these representations are not discrete, that they are interrelated, and that studying their relationships leads to greater conceptual understandings than we would otherwise have. For instance, a student can understand the value of written communication. They can compose a piece of writing and present that piece of writing in hopes of creating a certain effect. The same can be done with an oral presentation, or by using gestures or pictures. Multimodal learning challenges students to communicate in more than one of these modes, principally challenging them to think about how these different modes of communication can work together, thus pushing them out of the box of only considering each mode discretely. While the multimodal framework is incredibly useful in the specificity it provides, it is undergirded by a metacognitive framework; that is to say that the principles inherent in metacognitive theory are echoed in considerations of multimodal learning. Or, to put it another way, the multimodal framework is bolstered by a metacognitive one.

At the level of human cognition, we understand that human beings conceptualize information by classifying, or creating, schema for (this is also known as framing) that information and then synthesize an understanding of that classification by analyzing its relation to other schema.[3] To give an example, if one wants to create a cognitive frame for a new heretofore unknown color, say, baby blue, a color that is light blue in hue, one can understand that the color is a color, which is to say it occupies a space on the electromagnetic spectrum that is visible to the human eye, that it is a subcategory of a known primary color, which is blue, and that it can be further subcategorized into the classification of colors that are known as light blue, like sky blue, pastel blue, and powder blue. In the realm of metacognition, all the categories listed are frames and subframes that the mind must process in its understanding, or knowledge, of baby blue. To know what baby blue might be used for, one would then have to access frames that contain paint or sheets or drapes or eyeballs or flowers or butterflies. All of these also have subcategories and frames regarding practical and abstract use.

I mention this here because it is important for the teaching of podcasts for several reasons, probably the most obvious being that the more modes one can challenge a student to work in, the more likely they are able to understand the others given the amount of cross-over involved between modes. Though probably more importantly, students understand themselves as storytellers (which is in and of itself a frame as well as a mode), which is to say they understand that they are not just creating a story, but also that they themselves are a creator, which comes with its own set of principles, precedents, and classifications, and understanding this means that there can be no cognitive frame or schema within the creative process that is not directly related to the selfhood of the person who is doing the creating.

To put it another way, if the assertion that multimodal and metacognitive learning is valuable because it allows students to increase the number of cognitive connections they make, then one must assume that the student's identity is fundamental to that process as there can be no existing or potential cognitive frame which is not directly related to the student's identity. I imagine there might be some objectors who might want to point out that it is theoretically possible, in some abstract way, and in some abstract and/or speculative examples, for a person to create frames or schemas of understanding that are impersonal, which is to say they do not need to relate to the personality or identity of the consciousness that creates them, just as it's possible to create frames where the relation of the frame to the identity is negligible. It should be noted that these sorts of thought experiments erase cultural identity as a matter of course, and that one simply cannot, once they understand identity as a frame, preclude identity's relationship to all other potential frames. This is important to point out because it directly relates to large social issues concerning our creative writing classrooms, which too often operate under the base assumption that all students represent themselves in their work the same way, regardless of their individual, class, or cultural backgrounds, and this just isn't true. It can't be true, and the assumption that it is true goes back to creative writing department's roots in the acceptance of New Criticism where not only is there one true meaning of a text but also, and more importantly, at least for the purposes of this chapter, one true arbiter of whether a text is aesthetically "good" and "right." And, while this probably seemed useful to instructors trying to justify the existence of their departments fifty years ago, it has long since outlasted its usefulness. The obvious damage it's caused far outweighs any so-called practical feasibility some may argue still lies in the universality of the technique.

Student identity is an important consideration to be sure. And, in some ways it has always been an important consideration. The issue is that instructors often use the same sorts of traditional techniques that have always been available in hopes of helping students "find" their "voice." As has already been discussed in other chapters, these traditional methods often overlook the myriad of ways students engage in cultural signification. We have, in fact, reached a point where most instructors will readily admit this. The problem lies in asking instructors to alter models they are familiar with. This is an issue that Felicia Rose Chavez addresses rather well in *The Anti-Racist Writing Workshop*:

> The traditional model assumes that workshop participants share an identical knowledge of craft, and wields academic vocabulary as a badge of authority. The Traditional model silences the author during workshop while participants compete over what's "right" and "wrong" with the text. The traditional model exalts the workshop leader as the dominant opinion; they write on the author's text with the expectation that the author will revise comment by comment.

One of the many points Chavez is making here has to do with the mistaken idea that a college workshop is somehow a good representation of any given student's audience, or that it can be made into one. However, given the absolute abundance of storytelling forms and styles, the idea that students, and instructors, can be aware of them all and then give craft advice on how to cater to or please that audience is an assumption that needs to be revisited. This is especially true when considering the number of genres and forms that have been traditionally left out of the creative writing classroom, whether it be slam-narrative poetry, afro-futurism, or the magic realism born out of Latin American oral traditions, all of which I've seen introduced in the podcast portion of my creative writing classroom. (Note: this is a short list. The long list includes afro-pessimism, Black-love, fan fiction of all sorts, fantasy, romance, mystery, and science fiction in a multitude of forms and genres and cross-genres). There is, for some reason, though I find this bias is fading more and more every year, a proclivity for those in academia, instructor and student alike, to exult realist fiction as the standard aesthetic for representative selfhood, and to approach critique as such. This is silly. Any piece of writing is representative of the writer who produced it, and the sooner more students and instructors are made aware of this, the sooner creative writing classrooms will become centers of production that's more representative of their selves and the cultures they come from.

The way I run my podcasting units, both in my introductory course and in my primary focus course, allows students to forego a good deal of this institutional bias, partially because of the decentralized writer's-room process I use for workshop (it's one that doesn't silence writers, with a primary focus on asking the students to generate ideas that the creator asks for, and can feel free to use or not use, and a secondary focus on what the students feel is working well, and not so well, when considering the sound design *specifically*), but also very much due to the latitude and alternative focus the production of narrative podcasting provides.

Creating Storytelling Podcasts: A Brief Instructor's Guide

I'd also like to acknowledge that teaching creative writing is not easy. The amount of time the job takes is generally much more than is good for anyone trying to maintain a healthy work/life balance. Finding the time to rework, or to add, content to an existing course is daunting. Introducing content takes time not only in the preparation phase but also to practice as well as to master. I'm advocating the addition of narrative podcasts to syllabi knowing full well that, even if I can convince you to do it, it's going to take you a good deal of time, energy, and adjustments to do so. While I hope I've made the benefits clear, I'm going to use this section to lay out the scaffolding I use for narrative podcasts in my own classrooms. I currently teach two classes that incorporate podcasts. I teach an introductory creative writing course where narrative podcasts are one of many creative writing assignments. This is a single two-week unit where students must write a script, cast and direct voice talent, choose music and sound effects, and learn to use sound editing software in order to put it all together. The other course I teach is just on podcasting, in which I ask my students to create fiction, poetry, and creative nonfiction podcasts. For the purposes of this section, I'll be focusing primarily on the basics of narrative podcasting.

In my classes, students are given a great deal of latitude when it comes to creation. The only requirement being that they create a story (whether it be through traditional writing or through an oral storytelling process). As a result, some students use multiple voice actors. Others use only themselves. In doing this, in the cases of both traditional writing and oral storytelling, they learn to ad-lib (and edit) in order to smooth out their own dialogue. This results in a creative project where students see their personal voices highlighted, which is to say their actual voices become a necessary part of the stories they've created. To put it another way, they are asked to become active participants within their own stories, which ideally leads them to their own personal narrative discoveries. That these podcasts must be a certain length of time and must be shared with the rest of the class means that students must understand the narrative elements necessary to effectively tell a short story as well as be prepared for students to hear their writing and their voices, while also seeing and hearing the reaction of their audience.

Writing, Recording, and Sound Mixing

In his book *Digital Storytelling*, Joe Lambert outlines seven major features for effective digital storytelling: point of view, dramatic question, emotional content, economy, pacing, the gift of voice, and soundtrack. Point of view, dramatic question, emotional content, economy, and pacing are all features that most creative writing instructors are more than just passingly familiar. They are, with few exceptions, the basis for most stories, and we spend our lives as storytellers and as creative writing instructors asking our students to consider the ways in which these can be manipulated within their own narratives. One only needs to shift their understanding of these features to an audio-digital storytelling format to discover the concepts of "gift of voice" and "soundtrack," which then become highlighted as additional or "new." Together these features allow the storytellers more tools and/or opportunities to guide the listener's understanding of their story in new, varied, and unique ways.

I break down the narrative podcast medium for my students with the following framework: writing, speaking, and acoustic non-verbal elements. The writing portion is the base of the narrative. In my introductory creative writing course, by the time we get to podcasts we've been discussing issues of narrative all semester. The speaking and acoustic non-verbal elements would fall under what Lambert describes as "gift of voice" and soundtrack.[4]

I use the formal characteristics of voice as outlined by Andrew Bottomley because his articles provide a practical guide to acoustic storytelling as they've already been established in the field of radio drama.[5] I also prefer Bottomley's terminology to outline voice and soundtrack for two primary reasons. The first is that "gift of voice" suggests that one must have some innate talent to engage in audio storytelling (and one does not), so dropping "gift of" in lieu of asking students to develop their own voice technique is preferable. My interest in referring to "acoustic non-verbal elements" as opposed to soundtrack is again a practical one. The term "non-verbal" provides a clear separation between voice from music and foley (foley meaning sound effects). These basic elements are something people in our profession are less familiar with, but we all know them, if not explicitly, then intuitively. I ask my students to consider these when they are analyzing existing podcasts as well as for when they create their own.

Spoken Characteristics

Fundamental spoken characteristics of voice include tone, timbre, intonation, pitch, volume, modulation, accent, rhythm, and breath (a good contemporary resource to familiarize oneself with them is in James Alburger's *The Art of Voice Acting*).[6] I discuss with my students what all of these terms mean and how they contribute to meaning and composition. Breath is perhaps the most important one as what we do with our breath often tells people more about what we mean than our words do. Moreover, often what we do with our breath means more than the words we say. A short and by no means exhaustive list of things we do with our breath: we sigh, laugh, cry, yawn, grunt, stretch, and inhale sharply. In class, I use an example of this from a past student's podcast. The podcast is about a small liberal arts college student who makes friends with a "townie" at a nearby coffee shop. Toward the end of the story, it becomes clear that the "townie" would like to be more than friends, regardless of the fact that the student they are enamored with is already in a serious monogamous relationship. There's a line where the main character's roommate says, "I finally confronted him and asked him if he was in love with Jane, and he said . . . nothing." The two major voice characteristics to notice in this example are the one- to two-second silence before the word "nothing," and the way in which the word "nothing" is delivered, which in this case is enunciated slowly, several octaves lower, and with a certain tension that informs the listener that the friend is saying "nothing" because they cannot answer the question honestly and at the same time do not want to lie. This is an example where the silence before "nothing" further emphasizes the word "nothing" which has already been emphasized by the tone, timbre, and modulation. It also reveals something about the attitude of the character who is speaking, and this is one of the many ways I tell my students they can add their "own voices" to their characters as well as their narratives.

Non-Verbal Acoustic Components

The last major type that we discuss is the inclusion of various non-verbal acoustic components which they have to mix with their verbal characteristics. Non-verbal acoustic components present themselves in two subcategories. This is musical accompaniment (which also abides by the rules of tone, timbre, modulation, and rhythm) and foley. Musical accompaniment can either add to or undercut the mood and/or tension of the overall composition. I provide my students with an example, the podcast "The Good Doctor," in which the addition of ominous pipe-organ music acts as a cue to the listener that they might expect that they are listening to a gothic-horror story. For comedic compositions, one can use bright, bouncy music to undercut tension. I often do this when I create a short composition with my students at the beginning of the unit. Foley can add a similar grounding in mood or tension, such as the inclusion of thunder in "The Good Doctor" example. But it can also emphasize certain events or actions, such as the inclusion of a tone that signals the arrival of an email, text, or direct message (or, as my students so often like to do, one can add the sound of violent events in order to emphasize certain major tensions of a story, like a gunshot, or a raging fire, or the sound of a car crash). This part is usually the most challenging for students as they have to learn how to use the technology. However, there are sound mixing programs that currently exist that can easily be demoed at their most basic levels, and students today are savvy enough to pick them up quickly, especially when the technology is introduced along with short troubleshooting exercises.

Sound Mixing

The major portions of sound mixing begin first with recording. Along with the recording of voice, they must find music and foley. Depending on the student's desired effect for a specific element of their story, they then must mix these components together, though I should say that the mixing process is often an active process where students are writing, recording, adding, subtracting, and mixing different components/characteristics throughout the act of composition. The main mixing techniques I ask them to incorporate are fading, foregrounding, and layering. In their initial assignment, I ask them to use introductory music that they must fade out. I also ask them to consider what sorts of components and elements they might include to make this composition "their own." Layering and foregrounding are important in that their music and sound effects must be loud enough for the listener to register them, but quiet enough that they do not interrupt or drown out the verbal narrative. As I previously mentioned, the example I first ask my students to listen to is a hundred-word story, a drabble, by Jake Webb titled "The Good Doctor." Norm Sherman reads this story on his podcast, *The Drabblecast*. First, I ask my students to read it, and ask them to think about the sorts of images this text creates in their mind. Then, I read it to them, emphasizing major story elements as best I can. I then ask them to think about how my reading, my voice, alters their understanding. Then, I play Norm Sherman's version. An especially useful excerpt is "The doctor paced, laughing manically, as thunder boomed in the sky above. Torrential rain pelted into his inner sanctum. He didn't care. Disgruntled villagers with torches were storming up the hillside. He didn't care."[7] I like to use this example because there is no action described within the story that does not have some sort of foley (sound effect) backgrounded within the audio. This is to say that when one listens to the story, they can hear pacing, laughing, thunder, rain, an angry crowd, electricity, and the sounds of something monstrous groaning as it comes to life. Then I can ask my students questions about how the narration is altered or enhanced by its audio features.

(1) What does the narrator create with just his voice in terms of tone, timbre, modulation, accent, and rhythm? I ask them about Norm's voice. Is it flat, or is there a sinister immediacy to it? What about Norm's voice changes when he repeats, "He didn't care?"

(2) I ask them about the music.

(3) I ask them about the other foley: thunder, evil laugh, electricity, angry mob, bells, rain, monster groan, and flipping switch.

(4) I ask them if they can notice any fading, foregrounding, or layering.

(5) I ask them to think about the possibilities of what they might do with their own stories, and how they might personalize these stories, making them their own.

We then talk about how all these things come together to add to the richness of the narrative as a composition, often going back to relevant parts of the story so that they can relisten to all of the different elements in order to critically evaluate them. I then give them a short demo of Audacity, which is a free audio-mixing software program, outlining the basics of recording, uploading, and downloading. It has a learning curve, but it's not a steep one. Much of the ins and outs of Audacity can be learned by trial and error and by simply asking Google. However, if one would like to find a good primer for Audacity, I suggest Todd Cochrane's *Podcasting: The Do-It-Yourself Guide.*[8] This is where students must mix sound features and components, combine them, foreground and background them. External sound files need to be uploaded, and this is nothing new to anyone who has had to upload a file before. A somewhat tricky part is lining up the sound files in order to get them to properly play over, and into, one another. For instance, in some versions of Audacity, if you accidentally overlap two sound files on the same track (you can play two files over one another, they just have to be on different tracks), the program will stop playing at that point in the file. This is a very common mistake for students to make, and it can be very frustrating for them (i.e., they often think that the program is malfunctioning). There are also issues that can arise, again, in some versions of Audacity, from incorporating too many foregrounding and backgrounding lines. It is issues like this that can grind the whole process to a halt, and this is why the troubleshooting I incorporate at the beginning of the lesson (and continue to do throughout our projects) is so important.

I also provide my students with a host of websites where they can find a whole slew of duty-free music and sound effects, though I also encourage them to make their own. These websites can be found with a simple Google search. After this, I give my students their first assignment. They do this assignment in class on the same day as the demo. I find this goes a long way toward dealing with those issues of troubleshooting. The directions are simple:

(1) Write a short narrative (a couple of sentences to a paragraph) where a character does something, anything that makes a noise.

(2) They should then record themselves. Then find music and a sound effect and add them to the recording.

(3) Then they should mix all three of these things together to create a ten- to thirty-second audio story that they present by the end of class.

The value of this initial assignment goes far beyond just being a troubleshooting exercise, though it is very effective as one. This is because most students are afraid of podcasting by the simple virtue of the fact that the experience of listening to one's own voice can be jarring and uncomfortable if one is not used to it. I would like to pause to note that I do not force my students to record themselves if they do not want to, as we make a distinction between narrative voice/creative vision and mechanical vocalization. I make this clear and give them the option of finding and directing their own voice talent, and

I'll expound on this point later. Additionally, the activity serves as a low-stakes creative exercise in which learning to use the software is prioritized over any sort of pressure to perform one's personal and unique creative voice. Also, the motivation is simple, everyone has to do it, which in the space of the classroom helps foster a sense of unity and collaboration. After we've listened to everyone's thirty-second stories, I present them with their major assignment.

The major storytelling podcast assignment I give to my intro students can take whatever form they please. Collaboration is not required but is highly encouraged. The requirements for the assignment are simple. Their major assignment, when completed, should be about eight to ten minutes in length, should contain a verbal narrative element, should contain non-verbal elements (foley or sound effects), music, and an introduction (note: it's also fun to ask them to include a fake commercial).

I've had students create podcasts that have come in the form of gameshows, news-programs, journals of supernatural exploration, spoken-word podcasts, creative nonfiction stories involving campus and off-campus experiences, and episodic adventure series, to name just a few. Many students embrace collaboration, many do not. One of the benefits of collaboration is that students do not have to record their own vocalization if they cannot or do not want to. And I allow my students to get voice actors wherever they can, which means they can enroll voice talent from outside of class (usually friends), all throughout campus and beyond.

The recording process itself offers a multitude of varying challenges. For instance, since my students do not have immediate access to a studio, students must find a dedicated space to record, whether that's with their own laptop (or computer) or with one of the school's computers. I once had a student who recorded the first part of their narrative and then played it back for me to ask what I thought. I told them I liked the slight reverb effect they'd placed over it as it seemed to add an air of authority, and they responded that they didn't place any reverb over their narration, that they'd recorded it in the building's stairwell, and didn't even notice the reverb until I pointed it out. I then informed them that, for the purposes of continuity, they'd probably want to consider doing one of two things. Either they would need to record the rest of their narrative in the stairwell, or they would have to find a different space to record and restart recording their narrative from the beginning. Interestingly enough, they ended up doing the rest of their recording in the stairwell, and it turned out quite well.

Throughout this unit, students learn that just like there are specific narrative characteristics that control an "imaginative" image when reading the same is true for listening, and that there is a good deal of commonality between them. More importantly, by the end of the unit, students understand the value of their own voice from yet another mode, and therefore another perspective. Again, we spend our careers teaching our students how to guide the imagination of their readers. How do we get our characters to sound on the page like they sound in our heads? Or, in what ways can we use our voices to shape the imaginations of people not ourselves? This is just as true for audio storytelling, which is to say, how do we inspire our listeners to see in their minds what we see in our minds? When is this important and when is it not important? What do we need to incorporate to tell the story that we're trying to tell? What audio storytelling elements can we use to do this? And which ones are the best ones for the story they feel best represents "their" creative vision and voice? Also, this helps students understand the ways in which stories delivered in an audio format are different from stories delivered in other formats. This is particularly valuable as a majority of the stories we hear on any given day are relayed to us verbally. And chiefly, it is a format that usually highlights the student's actual voice, which in most cases literally places the focus on them as a storyteller, which in turn puts the focus on their language, their literacies, and their perspective in several ways written textual production simply does not. Moreover, it provides students with practical skills and knowledge that will inarguably be useful long after they leave the classroom and with implications that expand far beyond the realm of storytelling, that is, having experience mixing sound speaks to a possible skill that they would not have developed otherwise, one that has broad and far-reaching practical applications.

Conclusion

Assigning narrative podcasts exposes students to a multitude of differing issues. They learn that there are tradeoffs between written and audio compositions, and understanding one leads to a greater understanding of the other. They are, ideally, forced to make connections regarding their multiliteracies that they may never have otherwise. The base reasoning behind narrative podcasts is as follows:

(1) Learning across modalities provides students with a greater understanding of how narratives function, how the different modalities are both discrete and connected, what successful storytelling can look like, and how their own narratives can be represented within this space.

(2) It's practical, which is to say that students also are able to learn a practical set of skills: sound mixing, sound editing, directing, etc.

(3) It's related to the concerns of narrative craft and style that we all value so highly. Students learn the creative limits and tradeoffs inherent in each of these modes. And again, that specific compositions afford certain advantages and disadvantages over others.

(4) Their personal voices are highlighted, which is to say their actual voices become a necessary part of the stories they've created. To put it another way, they're asked to become active participants within their own stories, which ideally leads them to their own personal discovery of multi-literate/multi-perspectival modes of communication. These are modes that they engage in on a day-to-day basis as audio-based communication continues to be the dominant form of discourse in most of our daily lives.

Furthermore, narrative podcasting not only gives students a space to highlight their own voices when writing and telling these kinds of stories but also gives them a chance to see themselves represented in their stories. At its base, asking students to write a narrative podcast challenges them to write a script, use their voices, consider all sorts of audio characteristics and cues, and even consider certain visual cues all while being attuned to their intended audience. There is a naked and obvious pedagogical advantage, and value, in providing students a space for this sort of cultural signification. All of this coalesces into a creative project where, because they are challenged to write, cast, direct, and create their stories, students see their personal voices highlighted, which is to say their actual voices become a necessary part of the stories they've created.[9] In terms of modality, this is "representation of the self." In terms of metacognitive action, this is the frame from which all other frames should ideally connect. To put it another way, my students are asked to become active participants within their own stories, which ideally leads them to their own personal narrative discoveries, discoveries that they then share with their peers. Additionally, and as mentioned before, creative podcasts allow professors to privilege the oral storytelling and performance creative writing modes that have often been unwelcome in much of academia and are often valued in minoritized communities.[10] This helps expand the meaning of what it is to be a literary writer beyond traditional spaces generally preserved for dominant cultures.

Is the introduction of storytelling podcasts the only and true way to enact the much-needed institutional change needed within the creative writing classroom that many of us have been discussing intensely for years? Of course not, but it's certainly one way that instructors can begin to decentralize the classroom's currently inequitable power dynamics. These advantages are then compounded by the varied metacognitive and multimodal benefits. Lastly, there is a practical consideration here that must be stated. Narrative podcasting is a driving form of media within our cultural landscape, with creators and listeners numbering in the hundreds of millions, and it's a medium that shows few signs of abatement. As a creative medium, it's incumbent upon creative writing instructors to embrace the medium. It might even be argued, and I might even argue it, that we are, perhaps, a bit late to the game, considering the medium has existed for nearly twenty years. It is, however, better late than never.

5

Poetry
From Performance to Analysis

Billie R. Tadros

This chapter argues that the integration of podcasts in undergraduate poetry classrooms offers one pedagogical response to the ways that Martha C. Pennington argues digital media demand "redefining not only literacy but also culture, creativity, and the criteria by which cultural and creative products are evaluated."[1] I base my discussion in part on my experience using podcasts both as assigned course texts and as student assignments in undergraduate general education creative writing and literature poetry courses. I begin by offering an overview of some of the changes digital media are creating in literacy and creativity, and in "creative literacy,"[2] and by considering the implications of these changes for undergraduate creative writing and literature classes in particular. I extend Pennington's broader analysis to the undergraduate classroom to argue that new forms of literacy and creativity require us to redefine, specifically, the criteria by which we evaluate the creative products that originate in undergraduate classrooms, and by which we implicitly and explicitly sanction and prohibit both the evaluation and the creation of certain kinds of creative products in academic contexts. Ultimately, I present the podcast as a medium that encourages undergraduate students to practice what Pennington describes as "little-c" creativity, as well as to critically read and analyze "'Big-C' or 'high' culture."[3] The inclusion of podcasts in the undergraduate classroom as both assigned course texts (i.e., assigned reading and listening) and student assignments (supplementing written essays and assignments) represents a growing cultural acceptance and sanctioning of the notion that creativity is, rather than something exclusive and elite, something common and accessible. This has a number of positive implications, one of which is that, if instructors and institutions adopt podcasts and other forms of "little-c" creativity in our classes, we might find that there are a considerable number of prospective undergraduate creative writing students outside of our dedicated creative writing programs (and outside of the select few students in those programs for whom we might someday write letters of recommendation for applications to MFA programs). In other words, we might find value in we ourselves defining creativity, and, specifically, "little-c" creativity, more broadly. Assignments like podcasts not only encourage "little-c" creativity but also support anti-racist pedagogy, whose aims include "[d]esign[ing] democratic learning spaces for creative concentration" and "empower[ing]" students "to exercise voice."[4]

I conclude this chapter by discussing the five-minute poetry podcasts students in my introductory classes produce, and by providing my assignment guidelines and a heuristic for determining what kinds of podcast assignments might encourage analysis of both "little-c" and "Big-C" culture and empower diverse classrooms of poetry students to value their own "little-c" creativity.

The New Creativity: Culture, Literacy, and Podcasting

Some of the ways that digital technologies are changing both what we read and what we write, and how we conceive of reading and writing, include increased ability to produce multiple copies of texts, to access texts in a variety of media, to produce and store large texts, to use software to digitally create and alter texts, and to collaborate with other writers through different media in online spaces.[5] Changes in the ways we read, encouraged and mediated by digital technologies, are having parallel impacts on the ways we write, and current trends include shorter, more personal writing; a move from standardized language to abbreviations, play, and code meshing and switching; multimodal and multigeneric writing; and greater collaboration.[6] These changes in reading and writing have resulted in what Pennington refers to as "leveling" and "deleveling" in literacy, culture, and creativity, as digital media are "'leveling the playing field' by putting resources within reach of more people," and, simultaneously, creating opportunities for specialization, for "innovation and 'deleveling'" in the uses of these same digital affordances.[7] The effects of such "leveling" in particular are collapsing the distinction between "Big-C culture," which "refers to those products of human culture that are recognized as great works of literature, art, and music," and "the more mundane and less recognized products of little-c culture comprising beliefs, values, and practices," a distinction that Pennington explains "is related to a Big-C/little-c contrast often made for creativity."[8] These distinctions are "underpinned by tradition-bound, elitist notions of educationally, culturally, and genetically favored people," one consequence of which is that "Big-C products are often institutionalized with restricted access, whereas little-c products remain accessible and in the mainstream."[9] Pennington introduces a parallel "Big-L/little-l contrast for literacy," arguing that "Big-L literate practices are those that link reading and writing to high culture," while "little-l literate practices" are "forms of literacy that are linked to activities of little-c (vernacular or popular) culture and of little-c (everyday or personal) creativity."[10] Big-C and Big-L products in the contexts of creative writing and literature are also frequently elevated within institutional racism, "an institution of dominance and control upheld by supposedly venerable workshop leaders (primarily white), majority white workshop participants, and canonical white authors memorialized in hefty anthologies, the required texts of study."[11]

I would argue that the "boom in creative writing"[12] so many writers have discussed as a higher education phenomenon of the last two decades in particular (e.g., Harper; Healey; Pennington) warrants labeling another institutionalized Big-C/little-c distinction, which separates the Big-C creative writing classroom from the little-c creative writing classroom. Big-C creative writers are the ones we expect to complete MFAs (and now, maybe, PhDs);

to publish individual poems, stories, and/or essays in well-respected print journals; and to publish books with university presses or esteemed small, independent ones. But even in 2010, Healey notes, the same special annual issue in which *The New York Times Magazine* highlighted businesses' appetites for what Pennington might classify as little-c creative thinkers "remind[ed] us bluntly that the old idea of traditional publishing and reading [was] pretty much dying."[13] And it was in 2013, only three years later, that Healey acknowledged that, "given how unlikely the chances of any one creative writing student going on to a successful publishing career, any dream of actually finding a large literary audience would be, for most people, a profound delusion."[14] Healey argues, though, that creative writing students "are not nearly as deluded as some literary pundits make them out to be," and that what most creative students want is not a path to a Big-C career as a Big-C creative writer, but, rather, "access to a kind of cultural capital that's not specifically 'literary' but much more amorphously 'creative,'" what he defines as "creative literacy," or "the skills and experience that students can gain from taking a creative writing class that they can apply to a broad range of activities and jobs beyond the classroom."[15] It's the little-c creativity and creative literacy fostered in what I'll call little-c creative writing classrooms that is of particular interest to me in this chapter, and under that umbrella of little-c creative writing classrooms I argue we should include not only traditional creative writing "workshop" classes but also literature classes in which students learn how to read, analyze, and evaluate Big-C and little-c creativity and culture, and practice Big-L and little-l literacy. Podcast assignments in these undergraduate little-c creative writing classrooms, and, sometimes, arguably, the existence of little-c creative writing classrooms themselves, represent what Pennington refers to as "digital third spaces,"[16] offering students means for exercising new, creative literacies, and offering instructors opportunities to support those creative literacies and exercise anti-racist pedagogies. These spaces, Pennington explains, serve as "contexts where people feel less constrained than in other more traditional and institutionalized spaces" and as "arenas where new things can be tried and people can experiment."[17]

What Pennington refers to as "digital third spaces" are the "culturally hybrid spaces where communicators negotiate new meanings, new forms of representation, and new language responding to digital affordances."[18] Seemingly disparate forms like the podcast and the Instagram poem produced by popular "Instapoets" represent both the leveling and the digital third spaces Pennington argues allow for the creation of new literacies—and for little-c creativity. Many of the students who enroll in my creative writing poetry workshop classes and my introductory literature survey in forms of poetry, both of which serve general education requirements at my institution, have come to poetry through such contemporary, digital third spaces—through YouTube recordings of spoken-word poetry, for example, or through the digital work of Instagram poets like Rupi Kaur, "the reigning queen of the Instapoets," and r.h. Sin, whose "bite-size, pro-women works command a million followers on Instagram,"[19] writers whose work is divisive in part because their little-c creative and cultural practices have garnered them the kind of popularity that used to be reserved for Big-C creative writers contributing to Big-C culture and Big-L literacy. Because texts like YouTube or TikTok videos or Instagram poetry tend to be accessible both in the sense that students can access them at no additional cost beyond what they pay for the internet or mobile data, and in the sense that they tend to be concise and colloquial, students in my introductory courses (both the courses whose primary focus is *writing* poetry and the ones whose primary focus is *reading* poetry) tend to be a bit resistant, and justifiably so, to purchasing a "textbook" in the traditional sense, for example, an anthology of poems with accompanying essays on form, both because of the price tag textbooks may carry for just one general education course and because their prose tends to represent the Big-L literature and Big-C culture from which undergraduate students often feel excluded. This is especially true for undergraduate students of color, as Felicia Rose Chavez describes the Big-C canon as represented by such textbooks as also representing "a profound, ubiquitous silence: the nearly complete omission of writers of color in person and print."[20]

I've shifted primarily to assigning texts available through three open educational resources that feature the work of living writers: the Academy of American Poets (Poets.org), the Poetry Foundation's website, and the daily five-minute poetry podcast *The Slowdown,* first hosted by the 22nd poet laureate of the United States Tracy K. Smith and now hosted by the 24th poet laureate

Ada Limón. This pedagogical practice not only responds to student feedback in course evaluations of earlier iterations of my class, but also mirrors other educators' increasing efforts to assign open educational resources, and the practices of anti-racist teachers like Chavez, who notes that "[b]y the time [she] was in a position to design [her] own syllabi, [her] definition of 'anthology' had shifted from the traditional Norton to a curated course packet of [her] favorite texts, photocopied and bound by binder clip, showcasing historical and contemporary writers of color."[21] This practice also introduces students to the genre of the five-minute poetry podcast before I ask them to record their own contributions to that genre and digital third space, within which podcasts like *The Slowdown* (and others, e.g., *The New Yorker Poetry Podcast*, *Poetry Spoken Here*, and *Poetry Unbound*) illustrate the intersections between little-l literary and little-c cultural contexts and Big-L literary and Big-C cultural ones.

Poetry Podcasting: An Alternative Analysis

My focus in this chapter is on the results of a recent experiment over the course of the last few semesters in what I'd classify as a little-c creative writing class, my "Intro to Poetry" class, an introductory level literature course in which I introduce thirty-five students each semester to a survey of poetic forms through close readings of representative poems both canonical and contemporary. Prior to my experiment I required students in this class to complete three to five essays across the semester, analyzing and interpreting poems of their choice, but two years ago I began replacing one of these written explications with a recorded podcast.

Students enrolled in "Intro to Poetry" are often intimidated by analysis and interpretation—for many of them, my class is the first in which they've been asked to do this kind of close reading, particularly with poems as their objects of study. So the first week of the course I always have students read Edward Hirsch's essay "How to Read a Poem." In the beginning of the essay, he argues that

> [m]ost readers make three false assumptions when addressing an unfamiliar poem. The first is assuming that they should understand what

> they encounter on the first reading, and if they don't, that something is wrong with them or with the poem. The second is assuming that the poem is a kind of code, that each detail corresponds to one, and only one, thing, and unless they can crack this code, they've missed the point. The third is assuming that the poem can mean anything readers want it to mean.[22]

Toward the end of the essay Hirsch includes a number of questions students might ask of a poem—for example, "How is the form related to the content?" and "Who is the speaker?" and "Does the poem use unusual words or use words in an unusual way?"[23] I explain to students that if they answer one of these questions, their answers are going to be—or become—thesis statements, and the textual evidence in support of their answers is also going to form the support for their explication essays.

I assign episodes of *The Slowdown* (previously hosted by Tracy K. Smith and currently hosted by Ada Limón) that we then listen to again together as a class to introduce students to contemporary poems as they begin to develop a vocabulary for analysis, and to provide them with potential models for how they might complete their own explication podcasts later in the semester. Episodes of *The Slowdown* are five minutes in length, and the host generally offers a personal reflection on the poem that concludes in at least one explicit or implicit claim (or potential thesis statement) about the poem prior to offering a reading of the poem. Recently in this class I assigned episode #303, which features James Crews's poem "Telling My Father." In this episode, host Tracy K. Smith begins with a broad reflection on what love is, then moves to more personal reminiscences on and examples of love in her own life—talking about beloved friends and also a beloved pet, for example.[24] Finally, she introduces Crews's poem by name and says that she "read[s] it as belonging to the genre of 'coming out' poems," adding that she's "profoundly moved by the wordless gesture of love and recognition in its final lines."[25] The speaker in Crews's poem begins by describing finding and briefly talking with their father on the porch the morning after an evening the speaker has spent out, when the speaker is still "reek[ing] of . . . smoke."[26] The speaker's father merely says "Out late," smiles, and rubs the speaker's back before returning inside to the house.[27] The final lines to which Smith refers read as follows:

Later, when I stepped into the kitchen again,
I saw it waiting there on the table: a glass
of orange juice he had poured for me and left
sweating in a patch of sunlight so bright
I couldn't touch it at first.[28]

I told the students in my "Intro to Poetry" class that both Smith's categorization of the poem as part of a "genre of 'coming out' poems" and her articulation that the image in the final two lines represents love and recognition are, effectively, arguments, claims that illustrate her specific interpretation of the poem. In their own recorded podcast assignments, similarly, I invite students to engage with a poem in personal reflection and also ask them to offer at least one explicit or implicit claim that goes beyond summary and could serve as a kind of "thesis statement," a kind of engagement arguably representative both of more traditional Big-L literary analysis and of little-l literary practices like "vulnerable reading,"[29] as well as of little-c creativity.

Pennington argues that "[a]s students increase their awareness of the differences between little-l and Big-L conventions and practices, and the ways in which authors are meshing these, they will be able to make reasoned decisions about the extent to which they aim to fit their own writing into existing genre conventions, or to blend genres or break new ground for specific purposes."[30] What David Bell calls "podagogy," his "shorthand for podcasts-in-learning,"[31] particularly a "podagogy" in which students use podcasts for analysis and reflection, affords students in the undergraduate little-c creative writing classroom opportunities for anti-racist learning and little-c creativity that neither traditional literary assignments (e.g., written explications) nor traditional creative writing workshops typically provide. Dianne Forbes acknowledges that while "coursecasting," the pedagogical use of podcasts to transmit information, especially in online courses, "persists as the most widely promoted use of podcasting in higher education,"[32] in contrast, "it still seems relatively rare for students to generate their own podcasts" in post-secondary classrooms.[33] Using podcasts in the classroom not only to transmit information but also to "encourag[e] and enabl[e] students" to move from the receiving end of podcasts to the recording end in exercising and demonstrating their learning and reflection "corresponds with long-established work valuing student voice and the co-construction of learning."[34] This focus on student voices and student agency in the co-construction of learning is also consistent with anti-racist pedagogy.

Chris Cane and Annette Cashmore discuss a pilot study of 30 second-year medical students who developed podcasts relevant to ethical issues in genetics as part of a genetics course module, for which Cane and Cashmore evaluated "[t]he impact of podcasting on the students' learning . . . through a variety of methods" in order to "determine what effects the podcasting activity had on the students who produced them, both in terms of improving their understanding of the topic material, and also in developing their presentational skills."[35] They note that "[i]n the focus groups [formed to assess the effectiveness of the assignment] students commented that the process of researching material and thinking about how to present it to a non-specialist audience had broadened their knowledge and understanding of the topics."[36] Similarly, undergraduate students in my little-c creative writing classes tasked with creating five-minute podcasts analyzing and reflecting on poems of their choice for an imagined audience like that of *The Slowdown*'s, primarily of non-specialists, develop little-c creativity and transferable rhetorical skills. In particular, considering one's positionality and one's audience, and that "[l]anguage has meaning because it has meaning *for someone*,"[37] is understanding and exercising what Matthew Salesses defines as "craft in the real world," also crucial to an anti-racist pedagogy that acknowledges such "[c]raft is not innocent or neutral."[38]

Though I have primarily been discussing the implementation of podcasting in a little-c creative writing classroom that is classified in my institution's course catalog as a literature class (as opposed to a creative writing class), I am also working toward implementing a similar version of this assignment in little-c creative writing classes that are classified in the course catalog at my institution *as* creative writing classes. As Healey explains, at many colleges and universities where creative writing courses are increasingly in higher demand, "creative writing is becoming a *de facto* service course, despite being framed as a kind of extra-curricular or 'elective' course."[39] Healey argues that "[i]f students need both critical and creative literacy to survive and thrive in the 21st century, if academic writing needs to embrace creativity to remain relevant, then creative writing needs to see itself not simply as a training ground for literary writers, but as an essential point of access to creative literacy for the whole of academia,"[40] and I would argue that the five-minute poetry podcast represents an assignment that can provide such an access point in both little-c creative writing classrooms classified as literature classes and little-c creative writing classrooms classified *as* creative writing classes.

Though Healey concedes that "[m]ost students who take courses and even earn a degree in the creative writing field don't go on to become professional literary writers . . . this doesn't mean that they gain nothing from that educational experience," as these students develop little-c creativity and what he refers to as creative literacy.[41] These kinds of skills that serve as "an important complement to the still dominant critical mode"[42] are often represented in the course learning outcomes for both undergraduate literature classes designed to cover Big-L literature and those that promote little-l literacy and little-c creativity, and assignments like the five-minute poetry podcast can help students to achieve such course learning outcomes. Palitha Edirisingha et al.'s research has evidenced the importance of "a clear rationale that links podcasts" to other "teaching and learning activities,"[43] offering as examples of such rationales the development of competencies that also often represent course learning outcomes in undergraduate literature and writing courses, e.g., "essay writing skills," "reflective skills," "presentation skills," and "collaborative skills."[44] The five-minute poetry podcast serves such rationales and the development of these competencies, as students completing this assignment develop claims representing possible thesis statements ("essay writing skills"); analyze evidence in the poems about which they are podcasting, and are also welcome to share their own personal insights ("reflective skills"); present and record their discussions ("presentation skills"); and in some cases opt to work with one or two other classmates in completing and recording their podcasts ("collaborative skills"). In addition to these more traditional learning outcomes and rationales of literature and writing classrooms, the five-minute poetry podcast in the little-c creative writing classroom serves other outcomes and rationales too. Tracey Costley et al. argue that traditional approaches to writing instruction "fail to recognize the need in the current world to be continually innovating in response to rapidly changing student populations and conditions, including advances in media and writing technologies," and, thus, argue further that university writing curricular reforms should include "mak[ing] creativity and discovery central themes of the university writing course," "broaden[ing] the notion of the essay and incorporat[ing] non-essay and multimodal writing," and "center[ing] writing on students' personal, academic, and future professional/career identities."[45] Forbes notes that even in post-secondary classes that incorporate podcasting, "[a] fundamental problem" is an overemphasis on evaluating how much students learn using "a narrow view of examination results or test scores," and argues that, "[i]nstead, what is needed is a wider and deeper view of outcomes," which considers both "affective outcomes as part and parcel of learning outcomes" and "habits of mind in the widest possible sense," and which prioritizes "higher order thinking and deeper learning overall."[46]

In fostering little-c creativity, the five-minute poetry podcast not only broadens notions of what kinds of assignments instructors can incorporate into writing and literature classrooms and how they can evaluate student writing and creativity—thus, determining what kinds of writing and creativity "count"—but it also places *students* in a position to evaluate poetic products of both Big-L and little-l literature and literacy and Big-C and little-c creative writing—thus, determining what kinds of writing and creativity "count," a pedagogical practice also consistent with anti-racist teaching and anti-racist little-c creative writing classrooms. "What if participants themselves determined the course reading list, disrupting the boundaries between 'good' and 'bad' art?" Chavez asks, arguing that "[t]his is what it is to catapult the workshop into the twenty-first century."[47] In effect, this is one of the things that students do when they're given the freedom to podcast about poems of *their choice*, whether or not these poems represent previously assigned course texts. Some students in my classes do choose to podcast about poems we've discussed in class, sometimes poems that have been featured on *The Slowdown*, like James Crews's "Telling My Father" or Hanif Abdurraqib's "How Can Black People Write about Flowers at a Time Like This."[48] Others podcast about poems we've discussed as representative of specific received forms—for example, Elizabeth Bishop's villanelle "One Art" or Wesli Court's sestina "The Obsession" or Kim Addonizio's sonnet "Stolen Moments."[49] Others choose poems they've found outside of the curriculum but through the same open-access resources my syllabus draws from, searching the databases provided by the Academy of American Poets or the Poetry Foundation. Others still choose to explicate and reflect on texts they've encountered outside of academic contexts, texts like poems from Tupac Shakur's *The Rose That Grew from Concrete* or from Rupi Kaur's *Milk and Honey*, or Linda Ellis's viral poem "The Dash,"[50] which they've sometimes encountered in digital spaces like Instagram or Tumblr. Healey concedes that "[m]any successful students and teachers of creative writing are indeed skeptical" of the "democratization of authorship" created by digital third spaces and represented by many of the texts students, consequently, encounter outside of academic spaces, as "the field [of creative writing] often frames itself as the lone protector of literary excellence, especially given that the folks across the aisle in academic literature departments are mostly no longer interested in evaluating literature as 'good' or 'bad.'"[51] Healey cautions, though, that "it's too easy to dismiss creative literacy and, more importantly," that "dismissing it will not make it go away."[52] Additionally, dismissing creative literacy is tantamount to regarding only Big-C creative writing and Big-L literacy as worthy of academia, and only certain kinds of (primarily white) writers as worthy of authorship.

In comparing the traditional workshop model to the anti-racist workshop model, Chavez highlights the characteristics of the latter, which include texts that "are sourced by students and instructors over the course of the term, acknowledging that craft, form, and content are multidimensional and malleable," and says also that the anti-racist model "mak[es] meaning relevant and real" by "contextualizing . . . stories within a specific lived experience."[53] In talking about contextualizing stories within lived experiences she's talking specifically about "pair[ing] an assigned text with a conversation with the author, contextualizing their [the author's] stories within a specific lived experience,"[54] but I'd argue that there's also something to be said for asking students to contextualize their own readings of poems within their own specific lived experiences and within their broader cultural understandings, as Smith and Limón do in episodes of *The Slowdown*. In talking about evaluating student work in anti-racist creative writing workshops, Chavez argues that "improvement" in anti-racist evaluation "relies less on rubric, and more on participants' individual reflection on their ever-evolving technical, psychological, and emotional relationship to writing."[55] The five-minute podcast also supports students' individual reflections on their relationships to writing and on what they classify as "writing" or "poetry" or "art," as well as the development of their little-c creativity.

As part of a panel presentation representing early work on this chapter at the Association of Writers & Writing Programs (AWP) conference in 2020, I shared, with the student podcasters' permission, excerpts from two students' five-minute podcasts produced for my "Intro to Poetry" literature (little-c creative writing) course and some of their reflections on the assignment. One student, to whom I'll give the pseudonym "Pete," completed his podcast on Reginald Gibbons's poem "Hour," and the other, to whom I'll give the pseudonym "Elena," completed her podcast on Pablo Neruda's sonnet LXVI "I Do Not Love You Except Because I Love You." In Pete's reflection on the assignment, he shared that "[u]sing the podcast form rather than written format forced [him] to read the poem aloud multiple times to [him]self to practice for the final recording" and also that this "forced" practice led him to insights he might not otherwise have discovered just reading the poem silently: "While I read the poem aloud, I gathered information that I did not have prior, and [this] made me understand the structure and form of the poem more," Pete explained. One of the things I've found most interesting about listening to students' podcasts is the way their performances alone of their chosen poems represent interpretation. While some students are more comfortable writing scripts for themselves to follow verbatim in their recordings, and others choose to do that writing in real time as part of their recordings, students' voiced performances of the poems about which they choose to podcast represent layers of interpretation beyond even those that they explicitly acknowledge. Pete, for example, is a reader who, much like I do, prioritizes the line in his reading of a poem over the grammatical phrase or sentence that might extend over several lines. In other words, he'll pause at the end of a line, rather than at the end of a phrase, performing what Hirsch playfully calls "Creeleyiz[ing]" a poem, "paus[ing] at the end of each line" as Robert Creeley does in recordings of his work.[56] Pete made the assignment his own not only in considering the ways he delivered each line of Gibbons's poem in his performance of it but also in his choice to *grade* the poem—he gave it a B+—an evaluation that, in the context of his larger reflection and analysis, ultimately revealed the criteria Pete himself values and expects from poetry. Elena's podcast discussion of Neruda's poem (translated into English) offers a close reading specifically of the poem's diction and its use of imagery and metaphor—often contrasting images and metaphors she interprets as suggestive of the speaker's changing, even mercurial, feelings. Elena also balances this close reading with considerable personal reflection about how she herself feels about love and relationships. She states at the end of her podcast that the strength of what she ultimately reads as the speaker's "argument" is actually that "the speaker cannot quite explain why he loves this person, except for the fact that he loves her, as stated in the title and in the first line of the work." And she concludes, "And sometimes that's just enough."

I often tell students in my little-c creative writing classes there's a seeming irony about the ways that I teach analysis and interpretation: I insist on a separation of the speaker from the author—we don't assume the speaker of the poem is the author herself or himself or themself, unless we've got really compelling evidence to collapse the distinction between speaker and author, and my rubrics from prior semesters suggest that I significantly value "evidence" over feeling or even reflection. My course objectives have historically also reflected my desire for "evidence." One unwritten objective, though, is that I hope students will leave the course loving poetry, and its possibilities, even just a little bit. And I've learned that achieving that objective means allowing more personal reflection alongside the (other) "evidence." Though I first incorporated it as a potential one-off experiment, I've now assigned the five-minute poetry podcast for several semesters in my little-c creative writing courses. Each time students have found and read poems of their choice and talked about what they have meant to them, effectively expanding our course curriculum and our understandings of what "counts" as writing. And, to borrow a phrase from Elena, maybe "sometimes that's just enough."

Practical Applications: Poetry Podcasting Assignments and Advice

Edirisingha et al. report "an inverse relationship between the length of a podcast and the propensity to listen to it" in their research on the use of podcasts for learning in higher education, determining that "10 minutes seems to be the right maximum length that students are willing to listen to."[57] They argue that "[f]or the podcaster-developer, packing what you need into 10 minutes demands greater focus on the learning objectives and deeper thinking about content to achieve them."[58] While these guidelines are primarily directed at educators creating podcasts for their students, rather than at students creating podcasts for an imagined audience of non-specialists or for their fellow classmates, Edirisingha et al. offer evidence I can use to support my adoption of *The Slowdown*'s five-minute podcast model as representing the appropriate duration for demonstrating little-c creativity and sharing reflection and analysis often associated with Big-L literacy and Big-L literature classrooms. In what follows I offer excerpts from my assignment guidelines for the five-minute poetry podcast in my "Intro to Poetry" class, and a list of questions and considerations representing an annotated heuristic tool for determining if and how to use poetry podcasts in little-c creative writing classrooms, modeled in part off of Edirisingha et al.'s "10-factor design model" representing the "factors to be taken into consideration when developing podcasts to support teaching and learning in universities,"[59] and in part off of Cathryn Molloy et al.'s "[h]euristic tool for working with personal health and medical topics in RHM [rhetoric of health and medicine] research."[60] I intend to continue to consider this heuristic myself as I imagine other iterations of podcast assignments in my little-c creative writing classes, for example, podcasts in which one peer poetry workshop student interviews another about their work, podcasts in which students discuss elements of their own craft in conversation with craft elements they analyze in published course texts.

Excerpts from Assignment Guidelines

For this five- to ten-minute podcast you will offer a close reading and reflection on a poem of your choice. (You might, for example, choose a poem from an assigned class reading, a poem you find online at the *Poetry Foundation* or on *Poets.org*, or a poem you find through the podcast *The*

Slowdown.) You have more freedom with this assignment than with your single-paragraph explications in that I invite you to reflect on what the poem means, contextually and personally, to you, but in the whole of your discussion you should also offer at least one claim/argument that goes beyond summary, using evidence from the poem itself to support your claim. Because for this assignment you are considering a listener who doesn't have the poem in front of her/him/them, you probably won't verbally cite line numbers (the hosts don't on *The Slowdown*—you can think of Tracy K. Smith and Ada Limón's podcasts for *The Slowdown* as models for this assignment), but you should consider the most effective way you might provide evidence for your (at least one) claim. (You might use the podcast episodes on *The Slowdown* as inspiration. If you've listened to the ones I've assigned for class, and especially if you've listened to a few on your own, you'll see that much of Smith and Limón's discussions are personal reflection, but they generally offer at least one *implicit*, if not *explicit*, claim about the poem that goes beyond summary.) Like Smith and Limón do on *The Slowdown*, you should introduce and read the poem aloud, either before your discussion of it, or as the hosts do, after your discussion of it.

How "fancy" you get with these podcasts is entirely up to you. [. . . .] You can simply make the recording using a voice recorder app on your phone if this is what you're most comfortable with. You can also use Zoom to record and just submit the audio file from a Zoom recording. Additionally, you might check out the free phone application *Anchor* (anchor.fm/) or free software like *Audacity* (www.audacityteam.org/). The library website offers some good resources on podcasting.

You may, but are not required to, work with one or two other classmates on your podcast. If you choose to do this, everyone in your group will receive the same grade. (If you choose to do this, you can appoint one person to read the poem aloud, though all group members should engage in the discussion, or you can each read parts of the poem.)

Your submission for this podcast should comprise the following: a recording (.mp3,.m4a, or.wav format) of between five and ten minutes in length.

Annotated Heuristic Tool for Determining If and How to Use Poetry Podcasts in Little-c Creative Writing Classrooms

(1) Pedagogical Rationale

- What specific challenge is this assignment designed to address?
- How does this assignment serve the course learning outcomes?

Edirisingha et al. argue that because their research illustrated students' desire for a "clear rationale that links podcasts" to other aspects of a course, they believe "it is truly essential to make the decision to use podcasts in your teaching based on a teaching and learning problem, challenge, or issue that you have identified."[61] In my first use of the five-minute podcast assignment in my "Intro to Poetry" class, I sought to create an assignment different from the typical written explications I assign in the course, to diversify course content with assignments that might be more accessible to different kinds of learners, to provide students with less background in literature classes with a more casual opportunity to engage with explication and analysis, and to legitimize my decision to also assign poetry podcasts as course texts (i.e., as assigned reading and listening) by linking them to a graded assignment. My specific course learning outcomes for "Intro to Poetry" are that by the end of the course students should be able to 1. perform close readings of poems, examining their form, content and structure; 2. use critical vocabulary to discuss the form, content, and structure of poems in written work and in class discussions; and 3. develop and support organized literary arguments analyzing, interpreting, and evaluating poetry, using and citing textual evidence. Ultimately, I have found that the podcast assignment helps students to make progress toward all three of these broader course learning outcomes.

(2) Medium, Length, and Technical Specifications

- What technical specifications am I requiring, and why?
- How much facility do I have with the technologies I'm requiring students to use to complete the assignment? To what additional resources can I point students for help in creating their podcasts?
- How long are the podcasts I'm asking students to create, and how do the guidelines I'm assigning support my pedagogical rationale(s)?

Forbes argues that "[t]he main questions of relevance to student-podcasting are whether the technical challenges are realistic, and indeed whether the outcomes are worth the effort."[62] In part because I myself have limited facility with podcasting technologies, I permit students to create fairly low-tech recordings (e.g., I allow them to use just a recording app on their phones or their computers, rather than specifically requiring them to use software designed for podcasting like Anchor or Audacity). I've found that this makes the assignment less intimidating both for me as the instructor and for the students as podcasters. Additionally, I've found that this allows students to get creative in incorporating things like transitions and sound effects. Many students take the initiative to explore our library's podcasting resources and/or to experiment with software like Anchor or Audacity, while others experiment with what they can incorporate into a simple recording on a phone app—e.g., beatboxing, playing a musical instrument right next to their microphones as part of the real-time recording. Following my panel presentation representing early work on this chapter at the AWP conference in 2020, a number of other creative writing instructors, whose confidence in their technological facility was comparable to mine, were excited by the possibilities even of the simple podcasts I shared with student permission, and with the availability of free resources like Anchor and Audacity to which they could direct their students.

Gilly Salmon's admission that "[n]o one involved in the Informal Mobile Podcasting And Learning Adaptation (IMPALA) research studies" discussed in *Podcasting for Learning in Universities* "were ardent techies" seems to further support the pedagogical value of even low-tech podcasting in college classrooms.[63] "[A] podcast is a distributed downloadable audio file," Salmon explains, "[n]othing more" and "nothing less."[64]

(3) Author and Audience Positionalities

- What does the assignment offer students and their imagined/potential audiences?
- What models have I provided for students to prepare them to consider their positionalities and their audiences?

In their discussions of anti-racist creative writing pedagogies, both Chavez and Salesses emphasize the importance of diverse student voices and diverse student stories. Chavez argues that "whether or not participants identify as creative, their experiences are crucial to our collective narrative,"[65] and the personal reflections the five-minute poetry podcast invites provide one means of sharing those crucial experiences within an academic context.

(4) Evaluation

- Are my rubrics reflective of the pedagogical rationale(s) I've outlined for this assignment? Do they support the course learning outcomes?
- How am I evaluating and rewarding creativity?
- How am I evaluating and rewarding reflection?

Pennington argues that "[b]elieving that creativity exists in all human beings, and is moreover teachable and can be enhanced, is an important notion for writing pedagogy and for education more generally."[66] Assignments like the five-minute poetry podcast allow for such creativity to be taught and fostered not only in traditional Big-C creative writing classrooms but also in little-c creative writing classrooms.

6

Creative Nonfiction

The Sound of Truth

Rebecca Hazelwood

Introduction

One of the biggest challenges in every creative writing classroom is finding a way to move past the traditional workshop model, which is at this point outdated and perhaps even harmful to many students. The traditional workshop model is a product of Paul Engle's leadership of the Iowa Writers Workshop, and it has exerted influence on creative writing classrooms for more than half a century—despite the fact that it was created before the Civil Rights Movement and before the Stonewall Riots.[1] That is to say, it inherently prioritizes cis straight white male voices and demands silence of its participants. It reinforces the status quo.

The traditional workshop model has strict parameters: no more than fifteen students (though twelve is the optimal number), with the goal of workshopping one writer at a time as a class activity. During each workshop, the writer sits in silence while the rest of the class discusses their work. As Anna Leahy, Mary Cantrell, and Mary Swander note, there are specific reasons for this: "To minimize attempts to justify the work under discussion and to maximize introspection, the writer remains silent while the class discusses his or her draft."[2] Workshop participants are often directed to start with praise of the piece and end with critique. In theory, this model where the writer keeps silent is meant to keep the writers from patting themselves on the back for their successes and interjecting their intentions—rather than what is on the page—after critiques. Leahy, Cantrell, and Swander explain that the traditional workshop model "was meant to be tough and could save the writer years of individual trial and error."[3] The idea is that workshop participants can be objective only if they're discussing the piece without the writer's defensive objections.

But in practice, the traditional workshop is frequently described as harsh or "brutal," something to be suffered through without gaining much.[4] In my own workshopping experience, even when my piece had been deemed mostly successful, I often felt demoralized from sitting quietly for some part of an hour—sometimes even being instructed to keep my face impassive (an unfair and difficult request)—while others discuss my work's limitations. Even when I'm workshopping fiction, which is outside of my field and which I am eager to be helped with, it was difficult. I should also note that Engle decided upon this model for the Iowa Writers Workshop, which was then—and continues to be—only poetry and fiction. The effect of this model on creative nonfiction was never considered, and yet it is in place in creative nonfiction classrooms everywhere. But as Beth Nguyen argues in "Unsilencing the Writing Workshop," workshops are "always, always personal, no matter how often we're told not to take it personally."[5] You cannot completely divorce yourself from something you've created, and this is doubly true in personal nonfiction.

It should come as no surprise that this traditional workshop model has never worked well for creative nonfiction writers, who often use autobiographical material from their lives in their essays and then are asked to remain silent while others critique it. They have an even more personal stake in their narratives. Though many have somewhat successfully tried to "unsilence" the traditional workshop—Beth Nguyen among them—we need to push harder against this model. Thus enters the podcast in creative nonfiction classrooms, because it is the antithesis of everything that the traditional workshop model embodies. Instead of asking students to remain silent, the podcast gives them a voice. Instead of ignoring the writer's intentions, the podcast allows them to discuss their plans for their pieces, quite extensively. Podcasts allow the creative nonfiction writer to carefully consider their narratives because in the editing process, they become both writer and reader, speaker and listener. Perhaps most importantly, podcasts allow the creative nonfiction writer more agency.

Giving Agency to Writers

Countless writers of color have written about the way they've been silenced in the traditional workshop. In an essay for *Literary Hub*, Beth Nguyen describes her own MFA workshop experience after turning in a piece which mentions dim sum. Instead of discussing the piece, the workshop participants discussed what dim sum was and how it "must be something Asian"—and in the process they became completely distracted, not offering any helpful critiques.[6] Because Nguyen wasn't allowed to talk during the workshop, she had to sit through these micro-aggressions without even getting helpful criticism. She writes, "In this workshop format, the idea of what constituted basic knowledge did not include dim sum. They, the rest of the people in the workshop, decided what constituted basic knowledge."[7] In other words, the default of basic knowledge was white culture, and the writer's required silence—and lack of agency—reinforced this.

Other writers of color have written about the micro-aggressions of the traditional workshop model, including Junot Díaz, in his viral essay for the *New Yorker*, "MFA *vs.* POC." Diaz describes the faculty at his MFA as all white and the workshop atmosphere as one blind to assumptions about race and racism. Both the faculty and students revered work by straight white writers, which was not just the default but the aspiration. He writes, "Race was the unfortunate condition of nonwhite people that had nothing to do with white people and as such was not a natural part of the Universal of Literature."[8] The implication is that nothing else is important but the white experience, which doesn't need to be politicized in writing. Diaz concludes, "Simply put: I was a person of color in a workshop whose theory of reality did not include my most fundamental experiences as a person of color—that did not in other words include me."[9] Diaz's silence in the traditional workshop was reinforced by the silence about race surrounding him.

What we are talking about, then, is not just the way writers of color are silenced in the workshop but also how they are silenced—or shut out—by our perceptions of high art. In real life, I have seen white male poets privately bemoan the latest viral poem written by a BIPOC, and they invariably say something along the lines of, "That's not poetry." What they don't seem to understand is that they are basing their aesthetics—their very ideas of what poetry is—on centuries of poems by white male poets, never once considering that their aesthetics might not be universal. These same white male poets profess that they care about diversity, but it has to be diversity on their terms. They never realize they are biased. And these same white male poets are the ones leading workshop in a writing program near you. In *The Anti-Racist Writing Workshop*, Felicia Rose Chavez explains how systemic this white hegemony is: "When I speak of the traditional writing workshop model, I speak of an institution of dominance and control upheld by supposedly venerable workshop leaders (primarily white), majority white workshop participants, and canonical white authors memorialized in hefty anthologies, the required texts of study."[10] And this system continues to perpetuate itself every year in the number of books by white people that are reviewed in major publications, which then gain more attention and become books taught in MFA programs.[11] There is no escaping this system of white influence.

Many, including Chavez, have suggested ways to restructure the traditional workshop model. Chavez suggests honoring workshop leaders who are "effective allies to writers of color," with the preference for "superior teaching" over publications and awards.[12] Chavez also suggests a model that includes and searches for texts by people of color, as well as a model that "actively recruits people of color to participate in writing workshops regardless of whether they identify as creative" because their voices are important.[13] In all of her suggestions, Chavez is suggesting agency for the writer of color who has been stripped of it.

Nguyen, likewise, suggests a new model of workshop that "unsilences" the writer, actively asking the writer during workshop what they mean. In her workshop model, workshop participants prescribe less and question more, asking "Why did you use first-person? How important is the sister character supposed to be?"[14] This is instead of asking the writer to remain silent and making assumptions about what they mean in the text. Nguyen describes this as a transition from the writer being a passive receiver of comments to an active participant. She explains, "Rather, they become who they should be: the creators and navigators of their own work."[15] Though Nguyen is speaking from her experiences as a writer of color, this model gives agency to all writers.

It is this transition from passive to active that I am most interested in within my own creative nonfiction writing classes. It is this "unsilencing" I'm invested in. No longer do I want students to create in a vacuum, coming to workshop with no idea of how their words will be received, heard, critiqued. In a more active creative nonfiction classroom, which acknowledges the brutality of the workshop and shifts the paradigm from a white default, it's necessary to take "unsilencing" even further. The podcast is a great tool for this, one which actually gives the students a voice rather than being silenced. I am writing this in the middle of my journey to fully understand and implement the power of podcasts in my own classrooms. It is an act of trial and error, but what I am learning is invaluable to my teaching and I hope my journey can help other teachers follow their own.

In the past, I have had students record a podcast at the end of the semester, incorporating a passage of their own work, read by them, and some reflection. The idea is that they can hear how they are coming across when they are reading their work aloud. I have traditionally given them a lot of leeway, with very loose guidelines to make a podcast about creative nonfiction and read their writing. My syllabus from my creative nonfiction class last summer includes these instructions:

> This summer term, we're going to be expanding the horizons of our classroom and working on multimodal storytelling. That is, we're going to make podcasts for our final projects. Think about the great writing/storytelling podcasts you've heard: *This American Life*, *The Slowdown*, or even *The Writer's Almanac*. They all center on a work, whether it's a poem or a story, and they talk a bit about the process of writing, the history, or the context of it.

- Your goal is to produce a short podcast that includes your own writing (or a section of it, if it's coming from a longer piece) along with commentary about the process of writing, historical connections, or the context of it.
- Why are we doing this? Because we live in an increasingly multimodal world, and because there is no better way for you to assess your nonfiction writing than to hear it read aloud.
- You're going to be graded much more on content than the technicalities, because none of us are audio engineers and that's not what this class is about. However, I do expect you to strive for something clear, both in terms of content and sound.

And despite the imprecise nature of my directions, this has worked—likely because I was teaching a class of college seniors and graduate students. When I am teaching freshman composition, I have to include directions about what citation format to use, which font size and font style are acceptable, and even where to put their name and heading. If I don't tell freshmen these requirements, some of them won't even put their names on their papers. But seniors and graduate students need more freedom to create, even when they aren't used to the medium. I even tell them that they may do something outside of the few requirements I list, so long as they are making a creative writing podcast.

Last summer, one student asked if she could interview a local writer about her memoir—a narrative about leaving Vietnam after the fall of Saigon—instead of podcasting about the student's own writing. I said yes. In the podcast, which was turned in at the end of the five-week term, the writer reads part of her book, and then the student and the writer have a conversation about the real-life events of the book—including a very personal segment about the way Vietnam veterans were treated after they came home, how they were spat on and had food thrown at them. Near the end of the podcast, the writer says, "They need to know their service meant a lot to the Vietnamese people. They need to know that they made a difference, and I'm a testament to that difference." It remains the most sincere interview I've ever heard, one which reflected on not just why the book was written but also who it was written for—something that didn't appear in the pages of the memoir itself.

The podcast added another layer to the initial narrative, an extratextual thread of meaning.

Another student in the same class made a more traditional podcast, one featuring a reading of part of their essay and a discussion of their research. Their original essay successfully weaves together Albrecht Dürer, printmaking in an art class, and learning they had ADHD as an adult, but their podcast focuses on reading their essay for only a minute and then spends several more minutes discussing the history and contributions of Albrecht Dürer. The student explains that many people in workshop wanted to know more about Dürer. According to the student's podcast, we learn that Dürer was a German (Holy Roman Empire) Renaissance artist who produced woodcuts, oil paintings, and engravings. Dürer himself was one of the first adopters of etching, where a piece of sheet metal is scratched and has acid poured on it. We learn in the podcast that Dürer was deeply religious and sympathetic to Martin Luther, and Dürer's pen-and-ink drawing of praying hands has been reproduced widely and is found in many homes. The student's podcast is interesting and informative, but it does not take the place of their original essay, nor does all of this information belong in the essay—because it is a personal essay, about learning to focus while making their own prints. Dürer is incidental to the essay but integral to the podcast. So the podcast ends up becoming a different form of art in itself, related to the essay but not less than the essay, nor taking place of the essay. They are linked.

The podcast needs the essay to make meaning, but the essay also needs the podcast. They become scaffolding for each other, two parts holding each other up. And really, this is not so different from what the essay already does. Essays often become—as Brenda Miller and Suzanne Paola say in *Tell It Slant*—hermit crabs, taking the form of something else in order to protect their soft underbellies.[16] The spine of the essay—its form—often becomes another source of meaning making, as does the podcast. Truthfully, the podcast which is designed to have a student reflect on their own work becomes a different piece of art, one which is not just about reflection but art itself.

But as much as the reflection podcast works well as an end to the semester, I am starting to think that is too late, a goodbye reflection that is belated in assisting them with the work of the classroom. I want to be more proactive, to give students even more agency, so that in addition to speaking in their workshops, as Nguyen does by "unsilencing" the workshop, students start with their intentions via podcast.

In this new podcast model, the student writer hands out their work a week ahead of time, as usual, allowing their classmates time to read their work and comment on it. But then they have a second task before workshop, which is to record themselves reading a passage from what they think is the heart of their essay, as well as reflecting on what they are trying to achieve in their podcast. On the day of workshop, the student writer plays their pre-recorded podcast, and workshop starts on that note. Instead of the class picking the heart of the essay, the student writer picks. Instead of the writer waiting to be questioned, they start the discussion. In many ways, I've been doing this with peer review in my composition classes all along; I often tell students to ask their classmates about specific areas they're interested in, worries or anxieties or trends in their writing. "Be your own best advocate," I tell composition students. Creative writing students—especially creative nonfiction students—need that same encouragement, too.

Creative Nonfiction Podcasting

Students often come into the creative nonfiction classroom with two main problematic assumptions. The first one is that they think they have nothing to write because their lives are uninteresting. For traditional undergraduate students, this makes sense; at twenty or twenty-one years, many of them feel as if nothing important has happened in their lives. The second—and seemingly opposite—problem is students who think their narratives are interesting by virtue of their lived experience. That is, if they've suffered a miscarriage or survived cancer, their narratives are automatically interesting. They don't realize that "It's all in the art. You get no credit for living"—as V. S. Pritchett so famously wrote.[17] Interestingly, the solution to both of these assumptions is lively writing, for you can make anything interesting if it's written well enough.

Part of my job is teaching creative nonfiction writers that they can and must use all of the same tools as a poet or a fiction writer: vibrant language, images, storytelling, tension, rhythm, voice. Students must have a voice in their writing, just as they do in their lives, for "[v]oice is woven throughout the fabric of our existence, whether it's up close and personal, rendered in hot language, or cold type."[18] Voice is what makes a boring story about your day interesting. Creative nonfiction teacher Lynn Z. Bloom argues, "To develop their own style students need to slow the pace of shoot-from-the-lip instant communication and listen, really listen, to how they sound."[19] One of the ways to do this, of course, is to focus on both the figurative voice and the literal voice, to have students record their voices and edit them. Nothing makes you slow down and listen, really listen, as much as recording audio and listening to it over and over to edit it.

Because podcasts can only be so long when they're played in the classroom, maybe five to ten minutes before students lose focus, students must choose carefully what to record. In a dialogue about creative nonfiction with Jenny Spinner, Kate Dobson, and Lynn Z. Bloom, one of their suggestions for students is to pare the essay back to the essentials. Dobson says, "To tell the big story, write the small slice."[20] This makes sense. In my photojournalism career, I spent much of every day "feature hunting," looking for feature photos that were a "slice of life." None of these feature photos could contain the whole of a subject's life, but they were representative of who they were. These photographs succeeded if they had good light, composition, and a moment that meant something. In many ways, creative nonfiction attempts to do the same with words, beginning with what Dobson calls a "mattering moment."[21]

These mattering moments are what make creative nonfiction important—even if the moments are small. So long as they're told well, they are worth the reader's attention. In Brenda Miller and Suzanne Paola's seminal creative nonfiction textbook, *Tell It Slant*, they start with students' first memories and then ask students to zoom in on their five senses related to the memory. Miller and Paola suggest, "Readers tend to care deeply only about those things they feel in the body at a visceral level."[22] This is the only way to narrate those "river teeth," what essayist David James Duncan defines as "hard, cross-grained whorls of memory that remain inexplicably lodged in us" that are "moments of shock or of inordinate empathy."[23]

These mattering moments are the key to students' podcasts. Students don't have to have been divorced or lost someone they're close to in order to write these mattering moments. They just have to focus on the details. Often, creative nonfiction teachers require students to write flash (1,000 words or less) essays to learn how to focus on details. Bloom actually asks her students to write whole essays, as long as they want, and then cut their word count in half.[24] Another technique for accomplishing the same goal is assigning a narrative podcast of about five minutes. If a student has to tell a whole story—or slice of a story—in five minutes or less, they have to focus in a hurry. They also have to listen to their own narrative objectively in order to edit the podcast, and it's easier for them to see what details they're missing.

Of course, student writers can occasionally take these details too far. In one graduate workshop I took, one of the students wrote an essay bereft of details, lacking anything that would set a scene. So we told him this. When we workshopped his revised essay, he included every detail he could think of, including how many times he went to the bathroom and what he did in there. There was no reason for the bathroom details, no larger point being made, but the student couldn't distinguish between necessary details. However, I can only imagine that if he'd had to record his essay for a podcast, he would have been more judicious with his details about his bathroom trips. Reading aloud—even for an implied audience of a podcast—has a way of making us more self-aware.

In this way, podcasting can also help students who think their narratives are interesting just by virtue of the subject matter. I'm thinking of the many essays about cancer that I read while working at a literary journal, each of them written by the same person, each of them dry and dull. I always felt sympathy for the writer's experience, but I never wanted to pass the essay up for consideration. I wonder what the writer would have thought if they'd heard their own voice reading their essay aloud for a podcast. I imagine they'd hear their essay sink into tedium.

I'm also thinking of a student of mine who wrote about a miscarriage and told us of her tears and crying several times in the essay. The essay was well-written but for the fact that I noticed every time she mentioned tears and crying; because the writer had told me how she felt so often, there was no room for my emotions as a reader. I advised the student to read Dylan Landis's craft essay for *Brevity*, which advises "going cold" in an emotionally charged essay, or purposely leaving out most of the writer's feelings to give the reader space to feel.[25] Landis uses an example from Edwidge Danticat's novel *Breath, Eyes, Memory*. When a character named Sophie is sexually violated, Landis points out that Danticat describes the scene but leaves out the details of the violation and says nothing of the character's emotions. Landis writes, "So when Danticat skews cold [. . .] the reader's sense of horror on Sophie's behalf soars high, toward ten."[26] Landis describes this as "the clinician's coldness," writing, "It's the writer's description of those responses, not of the underlying emotions, that leaves a reader plenty of room to step in and feel the emotions for himself."[27] I would argue that if my student had recorded a podcast with her narrative, she would have noticed how often she mentioned her tears or crying; she would have caught it herself. That's what I want for all of my students: the ability to edit themselves. I want to give them agency.

Podcasts in the Larger World

The best part about asking students to create podcasts in the creative nonfiction classroom is that they already have so many models to choose from. In the beginning of their new textbook *Advanced Creative Nonfiction*, Sean Prentiss and Jessica Hendry Nelson make a case that "[i]n contemporary culture, creative nonfiction is a ubiquitous art form. We see creative nonfiction not only in our books, magazines, and journals but also in podcasts, documentaries, television shows, and on social media. When we craft our Instagram and TikTok stories, we construct a cultivated and curated social media story of self."[28] So it's no surprise that podcasts have exploded in popularity in recent years, including the first one that drew me in, *Serial*, the podcast that questioned whether Adnan Syed murdered his high school girlfriend. Of course, not all podcasts are about crime. They are often about narratives. Prentiss and Nelson categorize *This American Life, Radiolab, The Moth Podcast*, and *True Crime Garage* as examples of creative nonfiction, writing, "Indeed, most of our podcasts today are creative nonfiction, telling true stories in audio form."[29]

There are likely many reasons for the explosion of podcasts, starting with how bleak the news is; podcasts offer a lively alternative in a longer format during workdays and drives. Podcasts in the form of true narratives offer intimacy and nuance, an alternative to clickbait headlines and the popular digest. In his 1968 autobiographical work *Native Realm*, Czesław Miłosz writes, "Curiously enough, much is said these days about history. But unless we can relate it to ourselves personally, history will always be more or less of an abstraction [. . .] Doubtless every family archive that perishes, every account book that is burned, every effacement of the past reinforces classifications and ideas at the expense of reality."[30] Podcasts offer the antidote. They give all of us a voice, a democratization of narratives, for they are available for virtually anyone to start. All you need is a microphone and a computer—and they are one and the same these days—and access to the internet, all of which public libraries have. This may be an oversimplification of the resources needed, but if it is I don't think it's by much. My point is that all of the narratives which have been pushed aside and neglected for centuries have a place within the podcast world. It is my hope that my students will take stock of the abundance of voices and enter the podcast world with their own narratives.

7

Teacher as Podcaster

Kase Johnstun

In creative writing, as in all things, the struggle to create, the process itself, is as important as the finished creation. The process of every writer is different. While we, as teachers, do focus on process, it is important to realize that exploring the many possible differences in process is as important as the generalities we assume writers might share (or in some classes "should" share). Though often ignored, discussing difference is fundamental to student success as writers. In this chapter we will take an in-depth dive into the benefits of asking learning writers questions about their own experiences (with craft, process, publishing, revising, confidence, mistakes, and pitfalls), and then making sharing and listening to their unique and, sometimes, outrageously surprising and enlightening answers a focal point of the classroom experience. We will focus on how podcasts can help students engage in this way and even track their own changing views and answers.

The podcast is a unique and highly beneficial medium to answer the big questions about writers from writers themselves. It pulls the study of writing away from a textbook or, even, from structured, practiced, and edited answers which appear in the sorts of written and staged interviews we might use as supplementary readings in class. The podcast frees audiences and performers from pre-planned questions and a rigid time limit and allows for a more open dialogue about writing between writer and the host and, with hope, between writer, host, and the writer's literature on the page. Compared to other mediums traditionally used to teach creative writing in the classroom, the podcast is not only exploratory in form, function, and delivery but it also offers surprises and revelations that can only present themselves in a fluid, open discussion about craft, process, publishing, and that larger truth that lies below the surface of a writer's motivation. These revelations not only present themselves to the creative writing students but they also, many times, surprise the writer too, creating an "ah-hah" moment for writer and interviewer and listener alike, an unplanned reveal about a process or work that no one could have predicted before the podcast began.

The first question this chapter aims to answer: Why use podcasts in the classroom, particularly those produced by the teacher or students? The answer is simple: podcasts are unpredictable. The questions stemmed from honest and authentic conversation are unpredictable, the answers from those questions are unpredictable, and transparency of a writer's own revelations are unpredictable. This creates a lesson that is unpredictable and enlightening. It is an exciting way to engage students, who are more used to (and inoculated against) the predictability of the traditional class. And to budding writers, it can be refreshingly helpful to show that all writers are just fumbling around in the dark, a relief to the budding creative writer who feels like published writers have all their proverbial ducks in a row.

The second question this chapter aims to answer: What are the benefits of a teacher being a podcaster themself? First, I believe it shows budding writers that being a part of the literary community is important and that their work does not stop when they put their computer away. Second, well-designed and well-executed creative writing classrooms should be engrossing, illuminating, safe, comforting, and open. Having a teacher as a literature and creative writing podcaster, one that spends her life delving into the books, craft, and processes of other writers with the intent to be a lifelong learner—an infinite seeker of a new way to write dialogue, exposition, reflection, world building, and character development—creates a tradition of lifelong learning in the classroom and a culture of diverse, ever-expanding and ever-growing craft journeys. It also creates a space where students learn that asking questions is safe and good. That their job is not to achieve a point of knowledge which ends, but to be consistently open and curious.

Beyond creating a culture of lifelong learning and literary citizenship in creative writing, establishing early on that we, as writers, will always have something new to learn is important. If the instructor spends her time outside of the classroom seeking to understand the processes, publication histories, and craft techniques of others, this creates a necessary vulnerability in the instructor that, in turn, establishes an atmosphere of open dialogue where the creative writing instructor is not seen as the end-all and be-all purveyor of knowledge but as a conduit of knowledge to the expansive world of writers and their processes.

The third question this chapter aims to answer: Can the lessons learned from the instructor benefit the students in their podcasting journey? The answer is an absolute "yes," of course. As an instructor who is also a podcaster, experienced or inexperienced, lessons learned through the growth of a podcast can be invaluable to students who podcast in the classroom or hope to do so outside the classroom. As a writing podcaster, most specifically, these lessons learned from talking to authors on the microphone stretch wide and deep because, if I can be completely honest, writers are interesting, diverse, and unique creatives. A teacher who has an established podcast or has just begun a podcast can serve as a real-life navigator for her students, perhaps most directly as an instructor who can teach the art of a good interview, an important (and potentially paying) genre which often receives little more than an afterthought in the creative nonfiction section of a multi-genre course, if that.

As a long-time host of a literary and creative writing podcast, *The LITerally Podcast*, I hope this chapter serves as an opportunity to teach multiple lessons that instructors and students can integrate not only into their curriculum but also outside of the creative writing classroom. I hope I can share lessons I've learned from interviewing nearly one hundred poets, novelists, and memoirists over the last seven years and translating these craft concepts, lessons learned, and diverse approaches to writing lesson plans.

Successful Student Learning Outcomes

I must be honest; when I walk down the hallway, having just left my literature and English language classes, and enter my creative writing classroom, my entire persona changes. I move from instructor in front of the classroom in my literature classes to a cohort in my creative writing classrooms, a fellow writer who attends the class with just a bit more knowledge about the craft, about the industry, and about process of creative writing than my students, an instructor as lifelong learner. I believe this attitude in the creative writing classroom creates a safe and open space for all the writers in attendance. And I call them writers not students, even the freshest of them, because something so small and simple like naming them "writers" can positively change the entire culture in the classroom. It also helps them see the guests on podcasts as future selves, instead of unreachable celebrities.

Therefore, when I incorporate writing podcasts in our classroom as a way to enter into the creative lives and processes of published writers, students see their own interaction—their listening to the podcast—not solely as students but as budding writers engaging in the larger conversation of what it means to be a writer. The following learning outcomes are shaped for shared writer development through the medium of the open interview.

Reading and Listening Like a Writer

The first thing I tell my students when they enter my creative writing classrooms is,

> You will never enjoy reading like you enjoy it now because we will practice reading like a writer. Once you read like a writer, once you pull back the curtain and see every choice the writer makes and understand "what" the writer aims to do with her work through her motivations, craft choices, and their process, you will not love it the same way you love it now—reading just for pleasure—but I think you will love it more if you are really interested in becoming better writers yourselves.

Being a teacher and podcaster gives the instructor so many more ways to introduce her students to vast differences of writer techniques. They teach them through interviews with other writers what it really means to be a writer, what it really means to make craft choices, and what it really means to write with a specific process to complete their work. This transforms the "reading like a writer" lesson to a "listening like a writer," unveiling craft choices, process choices, and motivations choices.

Hearing the Authors Read Their Own Work

The first beneficial outcome of listening to an instructor-created podcast is the opportunity for students to hear authors/writers read their own work. With my podcast, as well as many other podcasts, the interview begins with the author reading something they've written. The reading time can range from three to fifteen minutes.

It is always enlightening and even thrilling for students to hear the writer read from their own work. This can be even more engaging if the instructor assigns readings from their novel, memoir, poetry collection, or essay or short story collection of the podcast guest. If the students are familiar with the author's work, then the reading from the podcast is generally guaranteed to pull students in. With familiarity comes admiration, and admiration opens the door to their curiosity. Additionally, when an author reads his work on a podcast, the author chooses what to share. This, in its own right, is very telling as to what the writer believes is some of their better work or at least one can assume that the work is of a quality that they feel comfortable sharing. Budding writers, having read the author's work, often wonder what the author might read before listening to the podcast, having already decided on their favorite passages or excerpts. In the classroom, this open discussion of what the budding writers want to hear can always lead to a lively discussion devoted to answering the questions "why" a certain excerpt spoke to them, thus leading to a larger discussion about what sorts of writing evokes emotion or engagement.

With literature and writing, the reader's schema plays into their interpretation of the written word. When an instructor and podcaster create a podcast about creative writing by inviting other writers on the show, she does it with the motivation to share the podcast with her students. This, in turn, shapes the questions that the podcaster asks, pointing those questions toward answers that will accomplish two major goals: examining the author's motivations and meanings in the text and illustrating the author's craft choices as well as their writing process. These two sorts of discussions can be enlightening to budding writers, mainly because guests' answers vary so widely across the writing spectrum.

Hearing the Author's Explanation of Their Story's Meaning

As a teacher and a podcaster, when I speak with my guests, I always ask multiple questions with the precursor explanation, "Many of my students listen to this podcast. What can you tell them about X?" This way, my guests understand my motivation for certain questions that are aimed to teach instead of strictly aimed for an enjoyable listening experience. By prefacing a question with the "teacher as podcaster" intro, writers do a very good job—many of them being teachers themselves—of adjusting their answer to fit the mode of instruction. This is especially true when I ask questions (mostly when chatting with poets) about the meaning behind their work. These are my students' favorite questions.

I always ask students "what do you think this means," demanding students cite textual evidence from the poem. During the podcast, I try to emulate this lesson by beginning my "what does this mean to you as the poet" question with my own textual evidence to establish a shared vocabulary with the writer and to show that I have read their work thoroughly before sitting down with them to ask them about it. For instance, with Sunni Wilkinson's poem "The Rodeo," a poem about place and love and local culture and loss, I will introduce the poem with snippets from her verses to not only lead her to the question of, "I see this as a poem about X. Am I on the right track?" but also give my audience and students an example of analyzing work with textual evidence.[1]

Many times, I am on the right path when I ask a writer about the poem's meaning, but many times I am way off track (students especially enjoy this scenario), but both paths lead to enlightening discussions about meaning from the author's perspective, leading to growth in the students' understanding of the great scope of meaning in writers' works. When I am on the correct path, this shows students how collecting textual evidence can lead to an even better understanding of a poem when the writer expands outward from the jumping-off point which I have introduced. When I am not on the right path, this leads to an even more enlightening discussion about what the author's motivation is behind the work at hand, which then leads to the author using their own textual evidence to explore those motivations, especially "how" they believed they achieved this through craft decisions.

Discussion of Craft Choices, Process, and Publication Journeys

Being able to ask the author about the meaning behind a poem or a short story or novel can be a fun lesson for budding writers, but some of the most instruction-worthy discussion comes from asking writers about their craft. I have discussed craft with more than fifty writers who have come on my podcast. I have also discussed it in person, listened to talks on it, and given talks on it for over a decade. Though many define craft as writers' "techniques" to convey meaning, plot, character development, setting, scene, and other elements in their writing, I more loosely define it as all the trinkets and gadgets that authors use to create a unique narrative, story, and voice. Others define craft as simply the writers' tools, but I find the terminology of tools to be limiting. I think the word "tricks" may be even closer, though it carries a negative connotation, to defining the decisions writers make to convey story. If there is one thing I have learned as a podcaster, it is that craft should be a flexible term, modeled by the writer themselves, as opposed to an inflexible list of rules that favor only one type of story, one type of poem, one force of creativity. I hope to help my students embrace the different, the unexpected, and their own cultural ideas about narrative through this looser definition.

Questions about craft, from the podcaster/instructor can be framed specifically to help student learners who will listen to the podcast later. I typically ask, similarly to my approach to questions concerning the "meaning," "I like to share this podcast with my students, how do you tackle X in your writing?" When asked this way, writers, especially those who teach as well, shift their tone to one of instruction, recognizing that they are no longer just having a discussion of their craft choices in the book, but they are also moving into an instructor role. Why do I believe it is important to shift tone and delivery by asking the craft question with the student as audience? I feel that writers make very specific changes to how they answer the question in the following ways that are beneficial to students.

(1) **They define their terms.** Many times, in writing (and in academia), writers and instructors assume that their audience shares the same vocabulary or jargon. When a guest knows that they may be speaking directly to an audience of budding writers, they will, most of the time, take the extra few seconds to define their terms. For instance, an author who is not speaking to students may say, "I use descriptive narrative a lot in my prose to move the plot forward while providing the necessary details of scene to give them a picture of the protagonist's surroundings." Knowing that the answer will be directed at students, however, the writer might say, "I use descriptive narrative, *showing details with lots of description while still moving the story forward,* a lot in my prose to move the plot forward while providing the necessary details of scene to them, *my reader*, a picture of my protagonist's, *my main character's*, surroundings." Of course, most students will know the definition of protagonist, but many would not know what the use of *descriptive narrative* might be. But since the writer defines both in her answer, the student does not get caught up in the vocabulary and can more easily digest the answer.

(2) **They give examples of their own curriculum.** While there are a few writers out there who do not have to teach to make a living, most have been teachers at workshops, conferences, or residencies. That said, many do teach or have taught and have created their own curriculum to teach craft to budding writers. I've had many writers who are also teachers on the podcast, and they have many, many great ideas for teaching craft and share these ideas freely on the show. This is not only beneficial to the students but very beneficial to the instructor/podcaster as well, giving her more options in her classroom to explore craft in ways that expands their curriculum too.

(3) **It shows their struggle.** I think this may be the most important lesson that writers can give when asked about craft. Many budding writers think they are the only ones who struggle with certain craft

> elements in their writing but asking the honest question about where more successful writers struggle comforts students because they learn that all writers go through similar struggles. In my writing, as an example, I must slow down and make sure to insert dialogue. Dialogue does not come naturally to me as a writer. I specifically like to ask other writers about which craft element they struggle with, and they always have very specific answers. Some may struggle with world building, others with descriptions, and still others with being able to finish a story or novel. These open and honest answers can only benefit students on their writing journey.

The discussion of craft can take wildly different paths, and we must recognize that one writer's craft choices may not fit our own. This is okay, of course, and being able to discern the personal nature of craft, where what works for one person may not work for another, is important for students who wish to embark on writing careers. This discernment applies to learning the process other writers use to get words down on the page. This way, different processes can be modeled. Students can be encouraged to experiment, to try some of the techniques discussed on the podcast on their own, to search for their own way with the help of those who have gone before them. This also helps students gain autonomy and a voice in the class, even if their own process falls outside of the parameters of what they may have heard they have to do to become better writers (e.g., Twitter is filled with rigid instructions which claim success is hinged on following one path perfectly, lest you "never become a real writer") The guests on my podcast help dispel such ideas and open the door for more budding writers to walk through. While all our processes are different, the question about process must be asked so budding can recognize there is not just one way to write, to finish a book or memoir, or to, quite bluntly, get words on a blank page.

One guest on my podcast, Deborah Reed, shared that she reads everything she has written on a novel before beginning her day's writing work, even if that is 200 pages. Another guest, Sean Davis, does the complete opposite and prescribes strictly to the sitting down and writing everyday methodology, while other guests can never imagine writing every day and only write in large swaths of time when they get the opportunity. Some, like me, write in the morning with coffee in a pitch-black house, while others wait until 11:00 p.m. to settle down into their writing, some with tea and some with whiskey. In over seven years of podcasting, I have never gotten the same answer to the question, "What is your process?" I find this highly valuable to budding writers and students frustrated by the endless lists on the internet which seems to provide a handful of generic answers that come together to really all mean the same thing—write every day or write 1,000 words a day or some other generic answer—but these lists do not begin to reveal the reality of the vast differences of writing process. Students must know this.

Beyond the open and honest discussions about craft and process, an open and honest discussion about the publication history, struggles, and paths of each guest is another highly beneficial lesson for budding writers. Many budding writers believe that those who have published do it with ease or have done it with ease in the past, and this could not be further from the truth. What students see publicly when it comes to publication—the awards, the press, the reviews, the smiles on social media—is almost always only the product of years and years of schooling, practice, rejection, and revision. Hearing published writers discuss their writing and publishing journeys provides students with two very important insights:

(1) **The journey is rarely easy or fast.** Students must understand that publishing, for most writers, can be years or even decades long. One guest, Adrian Todd Zuniga, also famous for his show *Literary Death Match*, spent ten years shopping out his novel, revising it, and shopping it out again before signing a contract with a publishing house. This is more of the norm than it is the exception, as five years of interviews have proven.

(2) **Though the journey is long and hard, it pays off with perseverance.** This discussion is even more important than the previous. If budding writers don't give up and continue to pursue the development of their craft, there can be a light at the end of the tunnel. Most importantly, however, it illustrates that we are all lifelong learners and that we must continue to try to be better writers with every rejection and submission.

Diverse Writers/Diverse Writing

In a creative writing classroom there is only one instructor. The podcasting teacher, by using his own podcast with his students' needs in mind, has the opportunity to share answers about craft, meaning, and process from racial, ethnic, gender, and socioeconomically diverse guests. When she shares her own podcast, newly created or well-established, with her students, and the teacher invites writers onto the podcast whose backgrounds differ from the instructor, I believe the diversity of guests offers two major benefits to budding creative writers. First, when students listen to authors who are different from themselves, this gives students the opportunity to explore the worlds of those authors through the authors eyes (and look beyond their own often narrow line of sight). Many students do not realize that an author's schema affects the way they see language, the way they see stories, and the way they create stories. These differences span all of the genres, and by sharing the work of those writers, students more fully understand that "writing" is not "just writing" and that background, race, ethnicity, sexual identity, and socioeconomic differences change how all writers see the world. This comes across in their poetry and storytelling. This alone is a lesson in itself, but the podcasting teacher—someone the students trust—can carry what they learn from the interview back to the classroom and meld it into their curriculum, expanding on what they learned from another writer.

In creative nonfiction or memoir, students have the opportunity to read about others' lives through narrative. The reading of memoir and creative nonfiction opens up a view into a world that budding writers may have never experienced or even knew existed, but beyond reading about the lives of others, the podcasting teacher can offer students even more. When played the podcasts, they are able to hear so much more than they would by just reading the prose itself. They get to hear about how the writer is able to deliver and share their world through writing; they get an inside glimpse into how the memoirist decided which of their stories were emblematic of their whole lived experience. When poetry is the day's topic, students are able to follow poets as they dissect their poetry in real time, as they share the poem(s) with listeners. It may seem silly to say, but word choice in poetry is key. Writers from different backgrounds see the world differently, so the words they choose carry different connotations based on their cultural identity and shared cultural beliefs within their community. Within the podcast, word choice can be broken down, opened up, and explained, which gives students the opportunity to grow not only as writers but also as humans.

Podcasting teachers who work to diversify their podcasts provide many "unseen" students with the opportunity to hear someone they can relate to on the other side of the microphone. When students see/hear a writer or author who resembles them, they recognize that someday they too could be interviewed about their work, process, and craft. As we have stated in other chapters, introducing students to diversity in podcasting and giving them a mirror to see themselves adds to the larger, much deeper conversation of writing and literature. In my opinion, it is our obligation as teachers (and as podcasters) to provide that mirror for budding writers.

The Benefits of an Open Discussion versus Written Craft Lessons

The most unique element of podcasting is the open interview/discussion format, intimately shared with listeners as if they too were in the room, engaging in the conversation around them. There is a lot to be gained from sharing open discussions on podcasts versus assigning readings about craft (though these are highly valuable as well and can be taught in conjunction with a podcast). The open discussion offers students more insight into the thoughts, perspectives, and authentic deliberation that circle inside the other writers' creative minds.

(1) **Pauses and breaks.** When asked a question, an author who wants to give their most authentic answer will pause and think about the question. This pause not only shows the student that the writer is doing their best to give the best answer but it also strays from any script the author may have practiced beforehand. An open question leads to an open answer, where a written craft lesson can be shaped and revised to sound perfect or performative.

(2) **Honest reactions to unforeseen questions.** Outside of well-formed answers and reactions to questions, the open discussion allows for the writer to react naturally to the organic back and forth between podcaster and writer. These reactions reveal the humanity of the author through laughter, grunts, long breaths, or any other non-verbal reaction. This humanity revealed through these moments gives students insight into the authors' voices outside of their writing, which many times can be more revealing than any other answer in the podcast. When a student sees a writer as just another human, the walls come down.

(3) **Digestion and digression.** I must admit that when an author begins to answer a question but then stops, thinks about it again, digests the question a little longer, and then digresses, revises, or changes their answer based on further introspection, it's my favorite part of any interview. This real-time diversion of thought can lead to not only some of the most enlightening answers for students but also a real-time revelation to the author. This real-time switch, change, or shift of perspective helps students see that authors are just like them, just figuring things out as they move through this writing world too.

The Art of a Good Podcast Interview

Interviews are never easy. Long before I did podcasting, I began interviewing people, first as a journalist for the Consumers' Association of Ireland, next for a small, community newspaper in Salt Lake City, and eventually, after a stint in publishing and editing, for the Tacoma Rainiers AAA ball club, but I never knew how challenging interviewing people about the hardest things in their life could be and expecting them to tear open their scars and share with me until I wrote a creative nonfiction book. I went to homes, I met people at parks, I bought coffee for people in crowded coffee shops, I sat in doctors' offices, and I ordered breakfast with them in a crowded NYC deli while looking at surgical photos and test results, silverware clanking on my recording and wait staff grimacing above us when the bloodiest of photos were revealed on the dinner table.

Interviews are never easy. This is a fact I share with students. I can't change it. I can, however, hopefully give students and teachers insight into why they are valuable, and if teachers and students are new to interviewing for a podcast, I can hopefully give them advice to avoid some of the mistakes I made while interviewing people across the United States.

I get asked a lot of questions about what makes a good interview (especially one designed to share in creative writing classrooms)? Isn't it all about their process? Won't interviewing someone else mess with the way I perceive their writing or even mess with my own process? These are very real questions and there's a very real motivation behind the asking. For the most part, I would argue that interviewing other writers about their process, craft, and publication history can only broaden the tools and skillset of the budding writer, which makes the podcast great for instructors and students alike. I also believe that the podcasting instructor, one that delves into the podcast arena with her students, showing them that the instructor herself is open to learning about other writers, their techniques, and their motivation, can demonstrate that writing is a lifelong learning art.

I have conducted interviews and been a part of interviews when the conversation between interviewer and interviewee fell completely flat. This happens. Many times, even if both of the parties have prepared for the interview, the podcast can fall on its face and never have the energy to prop itself up again. It happens. It happens to seasoned interviewers. It happens to new interviewers. And it happens to all levels of interviewers and interviewees in between. That said, there are multiple ways to prepare for a podcast interview that can hopefully prevent the conversation from falling flat, from living in a space of dead air, or from going south because the interviewee closes up.

Write a script. Outlines can be a podcaster's best friend. From my experience, just like when writing lesson plans for the classroom, I think interview scripts should be broken down into three- to five-minute, for a lack of a better word, chunks. So, if a student or instructor has a thirty-minute podcast planned, the script would consist of seven or eight scripted chunks based on seven or eight questions, leaving the remaining three-minute chunks for redirection, introduction, and conclusion.

A sample script might look like the following, each within three-minute chunks:

(1) Introduction, welcoming of the guest (three minutes)

   a. Interviewee's Response.

(2) A reading from the guest (three minutes)

   a. Interviewee's Response.

(3) Reading continued (three minutes)

   a. Interviewee's Response.

(4) Question about the reading or a question about the writer. (three minutes)

   a. Interviewee's Response.

(5) Redirection—if the interviewer asked a question about the reading in chunk 4, she could redirect to ask a question about the writer and vice versa. (three minutes)

   a. Interviewee's Response.

(6) A question about the writer's process. (three minutes)

   a. Interviewee's Response.

(7) A follow-up question about the writer's motivations with process (three minutes)

   a. Interviewee's Response.

(8) Redirection—a statement from the podcast enjoying certain aspects of the writer's work. (three minutes)

   a. Interviewee's Response.

(9) Ask the writer if there is anything else she would like to share. (three minutes)

   a. Interviewee's Response.

(10) Closing remarks (three minutes)

Aim to go off script. A script is extremely valuable, especially if the interviewer and interviewee are new to the format. The script gives gas and oxygen to the interview fire, if necessary, but, most importantly, it keeps the podcast moving forward. With that in mind an interview podcast will hopefully go off script. The best interviews do. While I do not propose going *way* off script because every podcast has its goals, I do suggest that budding writers and podcasters alter the script if the conversation organically changes course because this is generally when the podcast becomes most interesting. Change questions based on answers. Ask follow-up questions to answer that are intriguing. Recognize when the interviewee really enjoys talking about a certain subject matter and delve deeply into that subject matter, playing on his desire to really share or live in his passion for multiple chunks of the script. This is where the art of interviewing and podcasting really comes out, where it shines, and when real conversation and exploration happens.

Student-Created Interview Podcasts Lesson Plans

There are many ways I approach the practical application of the ideas discussed in this chapter. While students love the idea of interviewing others and being interviewed, as noted before, this, just like all creative writing techniques, takes practice, practice, and more practice. The following curriculum should take multiple classes to perform. I would suggest a full class period for each step in the interviewing process to illustrate how important it is to prepare for a podcast interview, even though there is really no way to fully prepare for how the interview will go because we all have our own voices, we are all unpredictable in our own way, and the true art of the interview comes within the ebbs and flows of the interview itself.

(1) **Lesson one: Read each other's work.** In the creative writing classroom, students are very conditioned to reading each other's work in a workshop setting. In my classroom, I always have students read for the positives first. Then I ask students to read solely to ask questions. There is no negative feedback in my workshop setting, especially in the undergraduate classroom.

While reading for the podcast interview, however, I ask students to read in the same manner with slightly different goals. They find the positives so that they can highlight aspects of the interviewee's work during those chunks in the script, and they read for questions about the work to flesh out their script.

There is a difference in the reading of a fellow student's work for workshop and one for the podcast, however. Within this setting I ask students to not look for holes or gaps within the text. Instead, I ask them to look for motivations and craft choices. This way, the interviewer does not aim to workshop the writing during the interview, but to instead delve into the writing in a way that is solely complimentary, solely aimed at treating their fellow student as a writer and not as a student. Beyond changing the format of readings to not feel like a live workshop, I feel this gives students confidence in their work, the feeling of being a writer instead of being a student.

(2) **Lesson two: Create their script.** In this lesson, I ask students to create their script. Before they begin, however, I share multiple podcasts with them. I share one where I had to stay on script, use every question I had in my outline, and redirect multiple times because the interviewee was nervous and answered in very short, truncated answers. This shows how valuable the script can be. Second, I ask them to listen to a Goldilocks interview where the script was used to begin the show, where the conversation became organic for three of four chunks, but the script was necessary again during the second half of the interview because the interviewee had exhausted his passion for the topic he talked so fluidly about in the beginning. Third, I ask them to listen to a podcast where only the first question in the script was used, but after that, the podcast went somewhere I could not have predicted but in a beautiful and organic way. I share this here to prepare them the best that I can for whatever can happen and to show them how valuable their script can be and to show them how to abandon it if necessary.

(3) **Practice.** In the classroom setting, there is no reason to have students go into a podcast interview without practice. In the end, as instructors, it is our goal to teach them, to give them the tools they need to succeed, and to also give them the confidence they need. I see no reason to throw them into the fire while recording for the first time, no need at all. Students are students for a reason, and they are in a creative writing classroom to learn, not to feel the pressure of being a professional podcaster.

I ask students to do two or three run-throughs of the interview. The interviewer and interviewee face each other as if they were recording, but there is no microphone and no camera anywhere in sight for this first run through. Next, I ask students to interview by running through their script the best they can, sticking to it and redirecting back to it if the interviewee weaves off track. Next, I ask them to practice again, this time letting the interviewee weave off track and see where the conversation takes them.

(4) **Assess the practice.** After the students have practiced twice, I ask them to assess the practices, asking the questions: (1) What felt good in the interview? (2) What felt awkward? (3) Where can we improve?

I like to take this step with the students because they find that—most of the time—they are on the same page and that they naturally both agree on the answers they find. From there, I ask them to make an early decision on how they believe the interview should proceed when the microphone is turned on.

(5) **Podcast.** Today, luckily, there are many, many different options for podcasting. There are many different applications and software to record, edit, and produce podcasts (these are covered thoroughly in previous chapters).

On podcast day, I ask students to dress up, to fix their hair, and to act as if the podcast were a job interview. I believe this sets the tone for the day. These days have become my favorites throughout any creative writing term when I teach interviewing for the podcast.

8

Audience and Publishing

Leigh Camacho Rourks

Conversations of audience in creative writing classes run the gambit from implied (wherein learning about audience is a product of the live conversations of an actual, if performative, audience in the workshop) to theoretical (e.g., discussions of Umberto Eco's "model reader"[1]). Unfortunately, "audience" is a notoriously difficult concept to nail down, a fact which is reflected in our differing pedagogical approaches. Still, it is probable that nearly all of our students have been told by a teacher (or, more likely, multiple teachers) to "consider audience" before they ever enter the creative writing classroom, and many of us use the term as such: one with which our students are already familiar. I certainly have, and I came to realize I was failing my students. I believe I glossed over the topic, happy to assume students' basic knowledge because I wasn't sure I had the tools to make the concept of audience come alive for learners in a way that turned the abstract concept into something immediately useful. I was just repeating my own education, where the term obviously had power, but no one really discussed what it meant in depth. I, then, like my students now, made little meaning out of the term and less conscious consideration of it.

In 1984, Ede and Lunsford wrote their article, *Audience Addressed/ Audience Invoked* because they believed that composition teachers needed help answering questions like mine—how do we make this abstract concept more useful to students and how should we approach it—especially in light of the conflicting advice coming out at the time.[2] Nonetheless, almost forty years later, a certain murkiness remains. In this chapter, we will discuss how to help our students connect with the concept in real and useful ways through podcasts, who the audience for those podcasts can ultimately be, and how teachers can begin to decide who it *should* be.

Microphone as Audience: Making the Conceptual Immediate and Concrete

The concept of audience is often harder to teach than we expect, at least in a way that inspires students' deep consideration of audience as a part of the writing process (as opposed to an afterthought). Jack Selzer points out that despite (or perhaps because of) earlier, traditional ideas (which are still at play today) of "audience" as a given, "audience has become fractured into audiences," with competing definitions and opposing camps for all the different ways we can define the term both as writers and as readers.[3] With such disagreement, it is likely that even two professors in a single writing department will have different views of audience and two different ways of teaching it to students, if either of them directly approaches it at all. However, despite disagreements, there is some consensus. It appears that students, like critics, "revise their concept of audience as they [compose],"[4] and that concepts of audience are, if nothing else, genre based.[5] Assignments designed to center the idea of audience should be created in a way which best facilitates a space to both discuss and experience audience as both a revisable concept and a genre-based concept. This gives us a beginning set of goals and, in doing so, allows students to negotiate their own locus of understanding between "real" and "imaginary" audience, addressed and invoked. In this vein, it is possible that the answer to the conundrum of pedagogical approaches to audience is to provide students with more room to build their own theory of audience. Therefore, we need to provide writers with practice within a genre where the concept of audience has immediacy, allowing students to experience the way genre can tighten our understanding of audience as a writing tool and to then focus on the ever-changing nature of this particularly abstract concept. Podcasts are a very audience-conscious genre, and thus are a great way to focus students thinking about audience in this way. There are two approaches available here (easily used in tandem or alone). The first centers on the aural text of public podcasts brought into the classroom as a teaching tool. We will begin there.

Since audience is "an overdetermined or unusually rich subject," it is best taught with honesty toward its complicated and malleable nature by providing opportunities for "analyses of precise concrete situations."[6] While readings certainly allow for these discussions, the concept of audience feels incredibly immediate when listening to a podcast. This may be due to the fact that podcasters and podcasting production companies display a hyperawareness of audience, utilizing an approach which directly and overtly acknowledges audience. This can have the effect of priming regular podcast listeners to think more consciously of audience. This is done through implied and direct usage of second person. Podcasts succeed in creating a "you" which feels less generic and more personalized, perhaps due to the proud embracement of niche audiences in podcasting as a whole (much different from the scattershot search for audience in other forms of media). Podcasters often speak directly to their listeners (especially those whose identity centers around the niche audience to which they cater). Here the use of second person is not simply invoked. but the word "you" is said to sincerely mean "you, my listener, you specifically." This functions as a direct, intimate invitation to a listener. For example, John Moe's *The Hilarious World of Depression*, which ran from 2016–21, regularly utilizes the word "you." In show promos, we hear, "Hey, it's John Moe. There are millions of people living with clinical depression in this country and around the world. If you've never had it, chances are someone you know has, a family member, friend, co-worker, neighbor."[7] In the introductions, we hear, "A show where top comedians talk about their experiences with clinical depression, to give some insight, make you feel less alone, and have a laugh or two."[8] Finally the conclusions to his episodes, which offer up the phone number for a suicide helpline for struggling audience members, begin with "if you or someone you know . . . ."[9] Listeners know Moe—their host, their guide—is talking to them, that he cares for and respects them—specifically them—the special listeners who share with Moe a specific connection to or interest in the topic of mental health. Moe's podcast is only one example of this very common audience-centered style in podcasting. It is a primary feature of the genre, a mode of intimate inclusion of the listener, signaled with popular phrases such as, "Join us" (which accompanies many podcast promos) and "our audience is curious" (commonly repeated in podcasting interviews). Not only does this allow students to analyze genre in terms of audience fairly easily but it also has primed those who listen to podcasts on their own to be thinking about audience when they think about podcasting. Students who listen to podcasts regularly engage in aurally intimate, repeatable, reliable relationships they control, choosing what relationship, topic, tone "fit[s] their current mood" and do so "without consequence"; these are the components that make up a parasocial relationship.[10] Additionally, due to the niche interests connecting podcast listeners to each other, our podcast-savvy students may experience parasocial relationships not only with the hosts of their favorite podcasts but with other audience members as well. The act of listening, here, is not as passive as with other media. It is hyper-intimate,[11] and hard to ignore.

The intimacy between audiences and podcasters is not just a matter of language and goes further than the experience of a parasocial relationship, though. The act of listening itself is an embodied act, where vibration creates resonance which, in *Intimate Listening*, Anna Jaakonaho argues has a direct emotional, cognitive, and social resonance for listeners.[12] Zuraikat also points to the embodied nature of the podcast, which most listeners experience through headphones (allowing the speaker to feel physically close) and, since podcasts are mobile, listeners can experience other external real-world stimuli from their own lives (e.g., while listening to a podcast on a hike) creating an "enhanced listening experience," which is extremely "immersive."[13] This means that listening to podcasts offers a kinetic learning opportunity where learners literally feel the connection between text and audience. It is a very powerful experience (such that academics are beginning to study the ways in which listening to fringe ideas on popular podcasts can dangerously deepen belief in those ideas)[14] which educators can use to reach students. It is also, then, a way the genre itself makes the concept of audience extremely immediate, allowing for the sort of analyses of audience Ede and Lunsford call for.[15] Interestingly, when listening to a podcast is utilized as a group exercise, the kinetic intimacy can both be at play and be disrupted in very interesting ways. According to Lydia French and Emily Bloom in "Auralacy: From Plato to Podcasting and Back Again," listening to podcasts in class help students move their primary understanding of audience from professor (the sagely writer they want to impress or, at least, get a good grade from) to the group.[16] This is an "aha moment" for learning writers: "When the site of audience reception moves from their instructor's eyes to their classmates' ears, students must also reorient themselves. They must shift their strategies, re-imagine their audience, and consider what role the media should play in shaping their rhetorical approaches."[17]

All of these ways that listening to podcasts can make students hyperaware of audience really enrich the classroom discussion. Since centering lessons of audience around podcasts, my students' participation in the discussion has moved away from rote conceptualization ("the audience is the reader") to true engagement, so much so that students sometimes bring audience up before I have a chance to. For instance, when listing to a podcast he didn't particularly enjoy last semester, one of my creative writing students blurted out, "Who is this supposed to be for?" The student felt that the podcast relied too much on specific knowledge of the author's book to be for a general audience, then relayed too many "obvious" tips to be for an advanced audience, and also used vocabulary he felt was overly advanced for a beginning audience. His understanding of the ways audience and genre interact was deep and he was revising his own understanding of what he felt the audience deserved in real time. Of course, these arguments could have been made had we read a craft essay, for example. But the nature of the podcast is so audience-forward that students can become very savvy about the concept very quickly.

That means that students can take this savvy from listening to writing fairly easy, parlaying their understanding directly from class discussion to their own writing process. Even when students are asked to create a podcast without being primed to consider audience through a listening assignment and discussion, podcasting provides a unique writing opportunity where audience is an inescapable, visceral, and direct idea. This is because in recording a podcast, the microphone (or computer or cellphone) acts as an immediate psychological reminder of audience. The technologies used in process and production function as audience themselves and are an integral part of the drafting of a podcast, creating acute awareness of audience through every stage of podcasting. Jason

Palmeri points out that "when a composer speaks into a microphone," she is given the benefits of reading out loud espoused by Peter Elbow: "the writer becomes conscious of how his or her writing 'is really a voice spread out over time, not marks spread out in space.'"[18] There is, though, more to podcasting than just reading aloud. Podcasting provides learners with the added benefit that the writer becomes her own audience, able to replay and hear her own voice as a separate entity when it is "produced by a machine and not her body," and, ultimately, can edit her voice in new ways allowing her to "resee the voice of her alphabetic text."[19] Because podcasting fosters a hyper-willingness to engage in revisionary practices, to foster a comfort with impermanence, it is a space that fosters, as Malcom Gladwell said of his own experience podcasting, "honor[ing] the conditionality of the work," especially in service to audience.[20] Audience becomes hyper-contextualized in this space. It becomes a multimodal consideration. The student cannot only read and reread her text, she can listen and relisten to her voice, and, most interestingly, in her software, she can see the soundwaves themselves and manipulate them. At every stage, learners are allowed to revise and at every stage they experience audience as a new thing. A student becomes her own audience, but she also experiences the hardware (microphone) and software as particular sorts of audiences themselves.

Broadening the Code: Audience beyond the Classroom

Of course, the podcaster is not an audience of one plus technology. Podcasts are made to be heard. This produces another benefit of using podcasts to help students consider audience. The fact is that even though creative writing classes ask students to, when writing, consider their audience more broadly than the class, students often struggle to see an audience outside their teacher and peers. There are many ways to overcome this, such as publishing discussions and a class journal. However, some teachers prefer not to discuss publishing directly and most others simply lack the resources for journal publishing. Even when we do, the audience tends to still be fairly narrow in students' minds: a university-centric audience. This university-based audience creates, as Jason

Earle describes it, the "narrowest code."[21] Earle defines codes as "the rules or conventions that govern different mediated forms of communication."[22] As such, they are writing conventions specifically attuned to the audiences of specific genres of texts. In teaching writing, the narrower the audience of an assignment, the narrower the code for that assignment. Earle describes codes for university audiences as being "low key" and lacking appeal[23]—certainly not want we want of student creative writing, but this may connect to the concern over lack of risk-taking in university creative writing classes, and it certainly makes discussing audience more difficult. This means the narrower the code the student feels is appropriate for a piece they are writing the less they are utilizing audience engagement strategies, resulting in a lowered understanding of audience as a part of the writing process.

This is problematic not only in a publishing (as many of our students may want a much more mainstream audience then academia, and even a literary audience requires a less narrow code then an academic one—though still narrow to be sure) but also in the sense that creative writing classes are not simply there for students who wish to be published. The idea of teaching creative writing as a way to bolster skills used in other professions is nothing new, but when students are primed to code their writing only for academic or even literary audiences based in universities, the benefits beyond publishing might be lost. Luckily, even if a student podcast will only be heard by the class, the genre of broadcasting, especially popular culture genres in broadcasting (such as podcasting), requires a broad code, which students, as consumers of popular media, are instinctively familiar with. This code is "community oriented,"[24] and thus more directly engaged in audience considerations. Thus, whether teachers assign students to write and produce podcasts to only be shared within the class or podcasts that the class itself publishes for a wider, outside audience, the benefits are similar.

Practical Discussion: Publishing and Distributing Student Podcasts

Perhaps the most difficult decision when asking students to create podcasts is to decide who will be listening to the finished podcasts. There are many options. Podcasting assignments may be designed only for the ears of the teacher, themselves. It is probably more common that the podcasts are listened to by the classmates of the podcasters. However podcasting assignments can also be designed for wider audiences, whether specific (the department or university which they were created in) or general (the whole of the internet). In order to decide, instructors must balance many considerations: first and foremost, the students.

The students I teach creative writing to tend to be smart, funny, creative, interesting, and self-conscious. Because I teach college students with learning disabilities, autism spectrum disorder, and ADHD, many of whom also have anxiety and/or depression, my concerns about student self-consciousness is, perhaps, higher than many teachers. Of course, not all my students are self-conscious, but it is a consideration I must center when deciding the audience for their podcasts. Because of this I never require my students to publish their podcasts more widely than the class, and depending on how personal in nature the assignment is, I may even only listen to them myself. That being said, my university is now building a radio station and a broadcasting class, and in future courses, I plan to take this into account in building my assignments.

If I were teaching a graduate-level class, I would instead create a public podcast whose episodes were made up of podcasts created by students every semester. I would do this because a part of professionalization for graduate creative writers is public readings and craft discussions. Advanced students engaged in making podcasts for a general audience are given a chance to design toward audiences of either their choices or their professor's. As part of the larger class discussion, teachers could require students to consider the difference between a pop-culture writing podcast, a performative writing podcast, and an educational one (broken further down into audience levels as writers). In doing so, graduate students will be forced to consider different forms of coding for audiences and will be better prepared as professionals.

Another consideration is assignment. A performative podcast of poetry or short stories or creative nonfiction is an assignment that lends itself to creating podcasts for broad audiences outside the course, while a metacognitive podcast may be better suited toward the intimacies of the classroom or even just the professor.

Conclusion

The question of audience and publishing is nothing new to those who like to debate the finer points of creative writing pedagogy. Many creative writing teachers have long placed publishing student work at the center of their course goals, whether this means asking students to submit work to the school's in-house creative writing journal, encouraging them to submit works to established external journals, or creating a class publication unique to each course. The question of publication has until recently been generally (and unsurprisingly) text-centered. With the rise of the DIY podcast and open platforms which will publish virtually any podcast submitted, so long as it adheres to community standards, the question has changed some. It is, after all, so very easy to publish a podcast to the greater world. However, the ethical, pedagogical, and practical considerations have not really changed, except in terms of scope. While unlikely, it is possible for a student podcast openly published on the internet to get considerable listenership, and even without this unlikely meme-like success, it is always a non-zero chance that a stranger may be listening in, exposing students in ways they may not be ready for or comfortable with.

Therefore, in making these decisions, we have to be very careful to consider who is sitting in our classes and what their needs really are before we finalize any decision concerning publishing student podcasts. However, the nature of the podcast means authorial considerations of audience will rise to the forefront of student's minds even without the push (threat?) of public publication. This is yet another reason podcasting can really help students engage with their work in new and powerful ways, not always so easily reached by traditional storytelling or poetics.

9

The Digital Divide and Podcasting

Leigh Camacho Rourks

Though podcasting is certainly a powerful tool to enrich and inspire students, it is, of course, not without its flaws. Most importantly, we cannot discuss the pedagogical benefits of podcasting without also confronting the problem of the "digital divide." Technology may seem like a ubiquitous part of all of our lives, but the truth is that "all of us" do not actually have equal access to technology. During the covid pandemic this reality became starkly apparent for even those far removed from the effects of what we consider the digital divide, as students across America were suddenly forced (for their own health and the health of the nation) into online classes that had not even existed the day before, and news reports of the strange and difficult mass transition flooded our screens. Amidst all the turmoil of the burgeoning pandemic, a critically large number of students and parents found themselves without the technology needed to support them and, as a result, an inability to access even the most basic learning tool: their teachers. From K-12 to universities, districts scrambled to find and distribute computers and tablets; families were left struggling and frustrated, and sometimes had the added hardship of an unexpected bill as children tried (and sometimes failed) to be responsible for the safety of technology their families could not afford in the first place.[1] In Palm Beach County, for instance, the local board of education implemented a county-wide policy which mandated that if a loaned-out tablet, laptop, or other device was lost or broken by a child, and their family could not afford to replace it, the child would be expected to do community service to "pay off" the debt.[2] If they fail to, the policy demands the children in question be banned from extracurricular activities,[3] a heavy burden for a child of any age.

The uneven distribution of technological resources in education is not simply a matter of devices. An even larger problem is access to fast, reliable internet. Even with borrowed computers and tablets, some students found themselves without access to an internet connection strong and stable enough to allow their inclusion in this new fully online national schooling ("60% of broadband users with lower incomes often or sometimes have connection problems").[4] Other students had no functional internet at all ("7%, accounting for 3.7 million households, had internet available sometimes, rarely, or never").[5] During Covid, what was once the "digital divide" gained a new nickname, the "homework gap" (with 30 percent of lower-income households unable to adequately and reliably finish work).[6] As the pandemic raged on and reliable access did not improve, we began to see the problem reframed again as a truancy issue, where frustrated students simply stopped attending. Some teachers (especially those with low-income students) reported "that fewer than half of their students are regularly participating."[7] Though this truancy could be due to a number of reasons, it is clear that technological inequalities driven by socioeconomic issues have had an outsized effect, the results of which has been devastating for many students:

> Titilayo Aluko, 18, a junior at Landmark High School in Manhattan, is one of the students trying hard to keep up with her classes who has been thwarted by her lack of access to technology. She has a district-issued laptop, but no Wi-Fi network in her Bronx apartment since her family had trouble paying the monthly bill. For classes like statistics and neuroscience, Ms. Aluko has tried to complete assignments and participate in video conferences using her cellphone, but that is sometimes impossible. "I actually need my teachers, who know me and understand me, to help me, and I don't have

> that," she said. "I just keep thinking, 'Oh, my God, I might not pass.' I'm just really scared for the future."[8]

Despite local and federal attempts to help bridge this divide, we will be slow to overcome it, if we can ever fully move past it at all. Additionally, I worry that as the extreme measures we took during covid subside, people who are no longer inconvenienced will forget all of those learners for whom this was not simply an inconvenience but a part of life, where modern assignments are always difficult in the face of digital inequality. This is especially true for all the students also attending schools whose technology and internet access lags behind our national expectations of "normal." Does this mean that technology-based assignments should be avoided? No. In this chapter, I will argue that the way we frame the "digital divide" needs additional scrutiny and that in the face of technological inequalities, podcasting is a uniquely accessible multimodal pedagogical tool, despite being technology-forward, which can be used successfully in many courses.

Inclusive Access

Digital inequality does not start and stop at the covid pandemic. According to the Pew Research Center, 15 percent of Americans are "smartphone only" internet users, and these Americans are overwhelmingly people of color, are from rural communities, and/or have a disability.[9] Many Americans, especially Black, Hispanic, and disabled Americans, have no traditional home computer or laptop. If we look closely, we can see the effects of digital inequalities in our classrooms every day. Even simple assignments usually require technologies many of us take for granted, such as word processing and printing. Online learning management systems (LMS) such as Moodle, Canvas, and Blackboard are no longer only found in universities and colleges; now, many school districts utilize them for every grade (though sometimes LMS use is more geared to the parents than the students). On the bright side, LMSs have, in recent years, become optimized for smartphones, but the assignments within them are often much easier for students to complete on a computer. It can be hard to write an extensive essay or lab report or novel on a phone, for example, despite how easy it might be to install the Microsoft Word or Google Docs apps. I should be clear here, though; I have students who are experts at composing, revising, and proofreading on their smartphones. Still, I have found this to be the exception, not the rule. Students with learning disabilities who also lack home computers/laptops are doubly burdened, relying heavily on accessibility applications on their phones that shared computer labs on campuses often do not offer. And, while research shows multimodal approaches are especially helpful for all minoritized students, many multimodal assignments often rely on technology unavailable to some of our learners. Without equal access to the technologies teachers can take for granted, students find themselves left behind.

However, statistics do not tell the whole story. One reason many people rely exclusively on cell phones, eschewing more traditional computers, is in their power—power we can and should harness in our classrooms. Thanks to smartphones, easier access to the internet has provided traditionally minoritized peoples across the world with a powerful tool to share their voices. In *Crossing the Digital Divide: Race Writing and Technology in the Classroom*, Barbara Monroe says the internet is an avenue for so-called "'have nots' [to] speak for themselves and, in so doing, . . . teach educators at all levels much about nonwhite ways of knowing and interacting in the world."[10] *Crossing the Digital Divide* was published four years before the iPhone came out, starting the smartphone revolution. Thanks to these pocket computers, Monroe's point is now truer than ever, and it bears considering. In a desire to right the wrongs of the digital divide, we must not succumb to the ways assumptions can further silence and minoritize students, and we must acknowledge the ways institutionalized racism colors those assumptions:

> The narratives about African Americans and the digital divide have displayed evidence of racist and stereotypical stories over time by disproportionately focusing on the access—or lack thereof—of populations of color . . . these concerns travel beyond research projects to classrooms, where learning opportunities are affected. Making room for continual growth and learning for all children may not necessarily mean installing digital technologies in every classroom, but it might mean reconsidering

> the ways African American children are using technologies—not as passive content consumers, but as active and creative content producers whose activities support and transform their own learning.[11]

There is, then, a danger in the current hyperfocus on the digital divide as synonymous with color divide, an idea which, despite problems like broadband deserts in predominantly Black neighborhoods, is an oversimplification which hides the truth. Tisha Lewis Ellison and Marva Solomon used counter-storytelling to study the ways in which Black families do in fact engage—richly and regularly engage—with technology. Their methodology relies on the fact that "counter-stories (a) bring attention to the perspectives of marginalized and silenced voices; (b) stand in opposition to dominant stories of privilege; and (c) resist and challenge opposition, racism, and classism, thus working toward the goal of social justice."[12] By collecting and examining counter-stories of Black technology use, the authors exposed the ways that the term "digital divide" has created a false binary that actually discourages some teachers from giving Black students helpful and enriching opportunities to explore their digital voices.

There is no singular "digital divide" neatly carving the world into easy-to-understand technological haves and have nots which we (without deeper inspection) perceive to neatly fall along racial lines. Teachers must find a balance between the fact that technological inequality exists, negatively impacting students in a number of ways both hidden and obvious, and the requirement that we do not hold back on educational opportunities for students due to a lack of understanding (or the willful ignorance baked into racist systems of research and pedagogy) of the nuances of technological use, access, and literacy within our student bodies (particularly BIPOC student communities). Marginalized students have been repeatedly failed by "traditional" teaching methods; letting our assumptions cut them off from newer methods is certainly not the path to righting those wrongs. In creative writing classes, perhaps our greatest wrong has been, and still is, silencing our minoritized students' voices, so leaning into work which can empower and boost those students' signal is imperative.

Ellison and Solomon's use of counter-storytelling brings up a point not to be missed: it is critical that we encourage our minoritized students to tell their stories themselves, that we make it clear their stories are welcome and needed and valid in our classrooms, and that we help make space for those stories in this world. If we look carefully, we will find that Black creators have done more than carve out a space on the internet for their voices, they are "active creative content producers," and they are everywhere online. In this book we have discussed bringing minoritized voices into the classroom through podcasts, especially using the many interview platforms; however, in making our choices as educators, we can think broader, do better. We can look not for minoritized voices given a space on mainly white, mainstreamed platforms, but for BIPOC content creators in spaces rich with BIPOC narratives, points of view, innovation, and, most importantly, power. Choosing podcasts made by BIPOC (for BIPOC) can uncenter the false narrative that whiteness dominates tech, leaving people of color floundering and failing to survive in the depths of the digital divide, and reveal to our students a world beyond the white gaze (or the white ear, in this case). This is also true for disabled content creators, Jewish and Muslim content creators, female content creators, and any other minoritized group you can think of and many you have not yet considered. The internet may not have brought about a democratized haven of post-racial equality, as some had hoped, but it is changing some of the ways gatekeepers hold power, and podcasting is one of the very direct paths minoritized writers have used to begin to wrestle power from the hegemony of traditional publishing.

This is not to insinuate that podcasting is a field somehow untouched by cultural hegemony. The largest podcasting platforms such as Spotify, Apple Podcasts, and Google Podcasts have outsized power and influence over which podcasts get noticed by their huge audiences, whether through Spotify's growing exclusive deals with podcasters who the company then prioritizes for audience discovery or through Google Podcasts' personal curated lists produced by their proprietary algorithms.[13] Nonetheless, Black podcasting audiences are growing very quickly, and they are demanding Black content creators that center Black narratives and Black voices: "61% say it is important that the podcasts they listen to include Black stories and perspectives. And despite the rise of networks like iHeart's Black Effect Podcast Network and the introduction of the Black Podcasting app, a majority (54%) of Black monthly podcast listeners wish there was more content around niche interests by and for Black voices."[14] We see similar listening patterns and desires across minoritized peoples, and vibrant communities of content producers answering the call and changing the landscape. In *Voicing Lived Experienced and Lived-Racism: Podcasting as a Space at the Margins of Subaltern Counterpublics*, Photini Vrikki and Sarita Malik see podcasts as a

> potentially radical space for counter-hegemonic discourses of meanings of "race." Considering that those at the margins of mainstream representation have struggled for decades to be able to represent themselves in the public realm (Eddo-Lodge, 2018, pp. 1–23), podcasts can make audible struggles for representation, challenge institutional colonialisms, and traverse both the political landscape and lived experiences of racialized oppression.[15]

Therefore, encouraging the listening to and creation of podcasts in our creative writing classrooms is an incredibly powerful way to not only fight cultural hegemony in our classrooms but also give learners the tools to continue the fight out in the world, simply by being a part of this creative revolution.

Practical Applications

Luckily, there are a number of ways podcasting is accessible for students suffering digital inequality. In asking our students to create podcasts, we do not have to ask them to have access to complicated recording software or hardware. They do not need professional microphones, pop screens, or mixing programs. They do not even need a traditional computer. Our most powerful tool as teachers assigning podcasts is the same powerful tool most of our students have in their back pockets (or under their desks while texting)—their smartphones. There are multiple podcasting applications designed specifically for smartphones that make podcasting easy and accessible, with buttons and menus that are easy to read and intuitive. Though I allow students to use any hardware/software combination they would like in creating their own podcasts, I show every class Anchor, a podcasting app owned by Spotify, which is not only free but is also so easy to use that I have my students trained in using Anchor in less than half of a single class period. It is very popular with students but some use other cell phone apps, and it seems like every year, the students bring a new one to my attention. I have even had students use the voice memo application on their phones, and while their finished podcasts lacked some polish, the ubiquitous, no-frills application got the job done. Even though I do some training in class, I provide students with a number of tutorials for reference on our LMS. As a result, I have yet to have any group of students unable to understand and use either a phone application or a computer program to complete the assignment.

I do regularly have some students who not only do not have a computer but also lack space on their phones for another application, have (rightful) concerns over downloading "free" software, or do not own a smartphone. Fortunately, during group work (and I do suggest making podcasting assignments group work when possible) only one member of a group needs to have the podcasting software on their phone. Some apps even support "call in" style participation for additional voices on the podcast, meaning students do not even have to be physically together to record and can do so using only one student's smartphone. In a pinch, I have even recorded a student podcast for one of my writers during my office hours (though I did make them "teach" me the software, to show they had learned to maneuver around it in class or could follow an online tutorial sheet). Still, I have only had one group ever need this additional layer of support, that honestly, required very little of me beyond my presence. In this group the student who had a cell phone lost it during the span of the assignment—these things happen. There are, of course, more powerful, more professional tools that some students may want to try out. I give classes a rundown of possibilities, but I always make it clear that I am not grading students on their access to a professional recording studio. I even make sure to play excerpts from podcasts with a strong DIY sound, so we can discuss how riveting writing, executed with care, can be more important than flashy equipment.

Unfortunately, our students are not the only ones who must contend with digital inequalities. Many schools lack classrooms with the built-in technology that listening to podcasts requires—most notably an internet connection and audio equipment linked to a computer. The simplest solution may be to assign listening to a podcast for homework, but the benefits of listening together can be lost this way, and students suffering from the same inequalities as the school itself will not be served by this "work around." Teachers who own smartphones themselves may find that their own phones have good enough sound quality and volume that podcasts can be played for at least smaller classes straight from their phones. If not, the cost of a pair of inexpensive travel speakers may be worth the investment. While not a fully low-tech solution, it is at least an achievable one.

Conclusion

We are best serving our students when we are keeping their circumstances in mind, which means admitting to ourselves that we simply may not know what our students' digital comfort, access, and ease are until we ask them. Therefore, designing assignments that require reliance on technology can be daunting enough that some teachers forgo assigning work like podcasts completely. This is not the answer. In a multimodal world, students whose educations function predominately in one modality (the written word) lose out, and our narrow understanding of digital inequalities may cause us to avoid giving minoritized students the kinds of assignments from which they could most benefit. Instead of avoidance, we need to prioritize an ethos of flexibility in both creating and grading technologically centered assignments.

Podcasting itself is becoming an excellent outlet for minoritized voices and communities, with audiences currently skyrocketing. For example, in 2021, Black audiences for podcasts went up 53 percent.[16] It is a publishing space that is more democratized than others, which means that if we are worried about changing the hegemonic face of writing and publishing, then we must not see our concerns over digital inequality as a reason to *stop* teaching digital storytelling and poetics, but instead to start seeing it as a reason to push the ways we teachers create access to digital creative writing, the ways we open the doors, the floodgates to the emerging creative renaissance around podcasting, especially for our students who would traditionally be silenced.

Afterword

Looking to the Future

Leigh Camacho Rourks and Saul Lemerond

Perhaps one of the hardest considerations when encouraging teachers to adopt a new technology, much less to reframe their pedagogical mindset around a whole different mode of teaching and student output, is whether there is enough staying power to make such an upset worthwhile. If the past is any indication of future trends, we can only assume that this is the case for the adoption of audio modalities in creative writing. Podcasts themselves are a growing industry. According to Nielson's 2021 research on the economic future of podcasting, the "Interactive Advertising Bureau (IAB) predict[ed] that ad revenue will hit $2 billion by 2023, well above the $842 million generated last year."[1] This certainly indicates a healthy and prosperous industry. However, even if the popularity of podcasts as we currently know them wanes, the audio landscape itself is going nowhere. We know more and more students are listening to audiobooks, supplementing class knowledge through podcasts, utilizing text-to-speech options (as well as speech-to-text), engaging in educational and professional conversations on digital platforms, and becoming full-blown digital creators in their own right. To keep up with them, we must become proficient in the ever-changing digital landscape, and the atextual creative experiences therein. Whether we look forward to the ways storytelling will continue to thrive as an auditory experience or the ways education will continue to need to provide multiple learning modes (and the many, many options in between), podcasting and podcasting-style assignments will continue to serve our diverse creative writing classrooms.

While we can't know exactly where technology is going, we do know that it is always changing, and changing quickly. Technology's only reliable constants are change and the fact is that these changes can and do fundamentally alter the ways humanity communicates and creates. Unfortunately, the paths of those changes can be hard to predict. When cell phones first became ubiquitous, few of us could have guessed there would come a day (and that day would come quickly) when no one would want to actually talk on those phones, preferring to text instead. Just as quickly we moved to image-based communication: first emoticons, then emojis, memes, and gifs. Now, we are recording speech-to-text messages, leaving our hands free to multitask. It is hard to predict what the next trend or stage of communication might be, but the option to record short audio clips as parts of texts and direct messages is showing up in many different applications, and students are already embracing this new modality. By incorporating podcasts into our classrooms (especially by having students create their own), we are giving our students the ability to be flexible and giving them skills to incorporate technology into their work. This multimodal flexibility can help assist them in navigating a landscape of literacy that is constantly in flux. So, when the publishing and writing landscape does (continue to) change, our students will have the plasticity to change with it, as well as the confidence to do so.

When we look at the needs of our students, there are other things we know with some certainty. We know our students should be aware that within the creative writing landscape there is an audio medium (represented in podcasts, readings, and audio books). It exists, and they need to know how their own work can exist within that space. Moreover, our students need to be made aware that *they* exist as individuals, as community members, and as learners within that landscape. Additionally, they must be prepared for the diverse environment that the audio landscape demands and accepts. We have the opportunity to help our students become the leaders and shapers of a literary world that embraces revolution in ways that traditional textual publishing has failed to.

Moreover, we know that we were not prepared for any of this. In the creative writing classes we took, the closest the courses came to acknowledging other modes of writing was reading a page from our manuscript out loud in our workshops. Neither of us even had playwriting as a component of our undergraduate or graduate creative writing courses, much less any sort of multimodal or digital genre instruction. Despite, finally, in graduate school being required to give readings, we were still offered no guidance or instruction in performing our own work. Although, like most others in our vocation, we became comfortable with the modality of public readings, guidance and instruction would certainly have helped professionalize us more quickly and imbue us with the sort of confidence which we only now really possess. Furthermore, since it's been demonstrated that multimodal instruction is a boon for people who are neurodivergent and those whose voices are minoritized, we both would have greatly benefited from such instruction, as we both often struggled in workshop, feeling like outsiders who might never belong. It is unfair to ask our past professors to shoulder this blame. Academia is as slow to change as traditional publishing, but the fact remains that we were taught as though there was only one modality and worked under the assumption that that single modality was the only modality we needed to know. We were wrong.

The future of writing has begun. The Covid crisis quickened what was already in motion. Readings moved online, and suddenly authors were expected to jump into the digital multimodal landscape we had mostly ignored. Audiobooks became even more popular, as did, of course, the podcast. According to *Writer's Digest*, "The audiobook market was growing before the pandemic, got a mega-boost during the pandemic, and is continuing to grow today even as we move away from pandemic isolation and regain a sense of 'normalcy.' And that growth shows no signs of stopping. Audiobooks are predicted to become a $19 billion dollar industry by 2027."[2] It seems like every author we know is expected by their publishers to go on podcasts to promote their books; while at the same time, there exists an expectation by readers that every new offering be made available in audiobook form. This is ultimately the case for all but the smallest presses. And while many authors may not perform their own books for audio publication, this growth means we must become extremely cognizant of the way, not just our poetry, but our prose, exists both on the page and in the ear.

It is difficult to imagine the world reversing this trend anytime in the near future. As a culture, we have recontextualized the act of reading. Consumers are beginning to see, and rightly so, little difference between reading a novel and listening to it, as are literacy experts. And, even when we as a society conceive of the two mediums as differently situated experiences, we increasingly understand the consumption of either as amounting to the same imaginative and intellectual act. Our students today are immersed in this recontextualization. Many listen to podcasts and audiobooks in their studies in much the same way past generations used CliffsNotes. Only instead of receiving the incomplete knowledge of a quickie pamphlet-style read, they dive into whole works (or complex discussions of those works) that they, like their predecessors, might have otherwise skipped. This is thanks to their comfort with the medium. Other students turn to audio literature as a tool, not in order to skip assignments but to read what, thanks to neurodivergencies, they might have struggled to get through before. Still others turn to them to expand upon their classroom studies or fill the gaps (especially in minoritized representation) that their formal studies leave behind.

Audio mediums will continue to be needed in the classroom simply because of the way they effectively democratize education, making it more accessible and improving the achievements of our students, no matter who they are. Moreover, true democratization of creative writing classrooms can lead to destigmatization in publishing. Our students are the future of publishing, and their vision is for a decolonized industry. By embracing multimodal approaches such as podcasts and podcasting, we hope to help our classrooms be at the forefront of these needed changes.

Notes

Chapter 1

1 Sarah Perez, "Spotify Says US Podcast Listeners Now Use Its Service More than Apple Podcasts | TechCrunch," *TechCrunch*, October 27, 2021, https://techcrunch.com/2021/10/27/spotify-says-u-s-podcast-listeners-now-use-its-service-more-than-apple-podcasts/.

2 Ibid.

3 Gavin Bridge, "Netflix Released More Originals Than the Whole TV Industry Did in 2005," *Variety*, December 17, 2019, https://variety.com/2019/tv/news/netflix-more-2019-originals-than-entire-tv-industry-in-2005-1203441709/.

4 Ibid.

5 Todd Spangler, "Netflix's Amortized Content Spending to Rise 26% to $13.6 Billion in 2021, Analysts Project," *Variety*, September 2021, https://www.yahoo.com/now/netflix-amortized-content-spending-rise-184211094.html.

6 "Spotify Technology S.A. Announces Financial Results for Fourth Quarter 2018," *Spotify Investors*, June 2, 2019, https://investors.spotify.com/financials/press-release-details/2019/Spotify-Technology-SA-Announces-Financial-Results-for-Fourth-Quarter-2018/default.aspx.

7 Ibid.

8 Hugh G. J. Aitken, "Allocating the Spectrum: The Origins of Radio Regulation," *Technology and Culture* 35, no. 4 (October 1994): 686, doi:10.2307/3106503.

9 Ibid.

10 "Hooper Ratings Summer, 1947" (C.E. Hooper Inc., 1947), https://worldradiohistory.com/Archive-Ratings/Hooperratings-Summer-1947.pdf.

11 Richard Berry, "Will the iPod Kill the Radio Star? Profiling Podcasting as Radio," *Convergence: The International Journal of Research into New Media Technologies* 12, no. 2 (May 2006): 149, doi:10.1177/1354856506066522.

12 David Honig, "How the FCC Suppressed Minority Broadcast Ownership and How the FCC Can Undo the Damage It Caused," *S. Region Black Students Assn LJ* 12 (2018): 44; Lili Levi, "The Four Eras of FCC Public Interest Regulation," *Administrative Law Review* 60 (2008): 813; Derek W. Vaillant, "Sounds of Whiteness: Local Radio, Racial Formation, and Public Culture in Chicago, 1921-1935," *American Quarterly* 54, no. 1 (2002): 25–66.

13 Honig, "How the FCC Suppressed Minority Broadcast Ownership and How the FCC Can Undo the Damage It Caused," 45.

14 Ibid.

15 Ibid., 78.

16 Ibid., 75.

17 "NPR Podcasts & Shows," *NPR.Org*, accessed February 12, 2022, https://www.npr.org/podcasts-and-shows/.

18 Tiziano Bonini, "The 'Second Age' of Podcasting: Reframing Podcasting as a New Digital Mass Medium," *Quaderns Del CAC* 41, no. 18 (2015): 21.

19 David A. Black, "Internet Radio: A Case Study in Medium Specificity," *Media, Culture & Society* 23, no. 3 (2001): 398.

20 Berry, "Will the iPod Kill the Radio Star?" 145.

21 Mia Lindgren, "Personal Narrative Journalism and Podcasting," *Radio Journal: International Studies in Broadcast & Audio Media* 14, no. 1 (2016): 23.

22 Tierney qtd. in ibid., 28.

23 Ibid.

24 Ibid.

25 Ibid.

26 Ibid.

27 Suzanne Keen, "A Theory of Narrative Empathy," *Narrative* 14, no. 3 (2006): 207–36; John Stansfield and Louise Bunce, "The Relationship between Empathy and Reading Fiction: Separate Roles for Cognitive and Affective Components," *Journal of European Psychology Students* 5, no. 3 (2014): 9–18; Taeyeol Park, "Engaging Students through a Podcast Assignment in Canvas LMS" (Society for Information Technology & Teacher Education International Conference, Association for the Advancement of Computing in Education (AACE), 2019), 1101–3, https://www.learntechlib.org/primary/p/207782/.

28 Carolyn Handler Miller, *Digital Storytelling: A Creator's Guide to Interactive Entertainment*, 3rd ed. (New York: Focal Press, Taylor & Francis Group, 2014); Joe Lambert, *Digital Storytelling: Capturing Lives, Creating Community*, 4th ed. (New York and London: Routledge, 2013).

29 Batya Friedman and Helen Nissenbaum, "Bias in Computer Systems," *ACM Transactions on Information Systems (TOIS)* 14, no. 3 (1996): 333–5; Wendy Lee, "Spotify Ramps up Podcast Deals with Influencers," *Los Angeles Times*, August 27, 2020, https://www.latimes.com/entertainment-arts/business/story/2020-08-27/spotify-podcast-deals-influencers.

Chapter 2

1 Craig E. Nelson, "Every Course Differently: Diversity and College Teaching: An Outline," *National Science Foundation Publication*, 1993, 93–108.

2 Ibid.

3 Anne Turvey et al., "The Many Voices of the English Classroom," *English in Education*, March 1, 2018, https://www.tandfonline.com/doi/abs/10.1111/j.1754-8845.2006.tb00782.x.

4 David W. Johnson, Roger T. Johnson, and Karl A. Smith, *Cooperative Learning: Increasing College Faculty Instructional Productivity*, ASHE-ERIC Higher Education Report, no. 4, 1991 (Washington, DC: School of Education and Human Development, George Washington University, 1991).

5 Louis Menand, "Show or Tell," *The New Yorker*, accessed October 4, 2020, https://www.newyorker.com/magazine/2009/06/08/show-or-tell.

6 Mark McGurl, *The Program Era: Postwar Fiction and the Rise of Creative Writing*, 1st Harvard University Press pbk ed. (Cambridge, MA: Harvard University Press, 2011).

7 Ibid.

8 Felicia Rose Chavez, *The Anti-Racist Writing Workshop: Decolonizing the Creative Classroom* (Chicago: Haymarket Books, 2021).

9 Ibid.

10 Ibid.

11 Junot Díaz, "MFA *vs.* POC," *The New Yorker*, April 30, 2014, https://www.newyorker.com/books/page-turner/mfa-vs-poc.

12 Ibid.

13 Beth Nguyen, "Unsilencing the Writing Workshop ‹ Literary Hub," *LitHub*, April 3, 2019, https://lithub.com/unsilencing-the-writing-workshop/.

14 Jimin Han, "Jimin Han on Rethinking the CW Workshop," *Pleiades Magazine*, 2015, https://pleiadesmag.com/jimin-han-on-rethinking-the-cw-workshop/.

15 Matthew Salesses, "When Defending Your Writing Becomes Defending Yourself," *NPR*, July 20, 2014, https://www.npr.org/sections/codeswitch/2014/07/20/313158511/salesses-writers-workshop-diversity.

16 Chavez, *The Anti-Racist Writing Workshop*.

17 Leslie Davis and Richard Fry, "College Faculty Still Far Less Diverse than Students in Race, Ethnicity | Pew Research Center," *Pew Research Center*, July 31, 2019, https://www.pewresearch.org/fact-tank/2019/07/31/us-college-faculty-student-diversity/.

18 Julie Botticello, "Engaging Many Voices for Inclusivity in Higher Education," May 26, 2020, doi:10.15123/uel.8805x.

19 Mary E. Hoeft, "Why University Students Don't Read: What Professors Can Do To Increase Compliance," *International Journal for the Scholarship of Teaching and Learning* 6, no. 2 (July 1, 2012), doi:10.20429/ijsotl.2012.060212.

20 Carey Jewitt, "Multimodality and Literacy in School Classrooms," *Review of Research in Education* 32, no. 1 (February 2008): 245, doi:10.3102/0091732X07310586.

21 Iben Have and Birgitte Stougaard Pedersen, "Reading Audiobooks," in *Beyond Media Borders, Volume 1: Intermedial Relations among Multimodal Media*, ed. Lars Elleström (Cham: Springer International Publishing, 2021), 203, doi:10.1007/978-3-030-49679-1.

22 Ibid.

23 Stine Nørkjær Nielsen, René Holm Andersen, and Susanne Dau, "Podcast as a Learning Media in Higher Education," in *Proceedings of the European Conference on E-Learning*, 2018, 424.

24 Francis J. Buckley, *Team Teaching: What, Why, and How?* (Thousand Oaks, CA: SAGE Publications, Inc, 2000), 13, https://search.ebscohost.com/login.aspx?direct=true&db=nlebk&AN=474657&site=eds-live.

25 Ibid.

Chapter 3

1 Jason Palmeri, *Remixing Composition: A History of Multimodal Writing Pedagogy* (Carbondale, Edwardsville, and Indiana: SIU Press, 2012).

2 Peter Elbow, "Reading Out Loud to Improve Writing," *Peter Elbow: The Democratization of Writing*, accessed December 10, 2021, https://peterelbow.com/handouts.html.

3 Peter Elbow, "What Do We Mean When We Talk about Voice in Texts?," *Voices on Voice: Perspectives, Definitions, Inquiry*, January 1, 1994, 1–35.

4 Ibid.

5 Raffaella Negretti and Lisa McGrath, "Scaffolding Genre Knowledge and Metacognition: Insights from an L2 Doctoral Research Writing Course," *Journal of Second Language Writing* 40 (June 2018): 12–31, doi:10.1016/j.jslw.2017.12.002.

6 Nielsen, Andersen, and Dau, "Podcast as a Learning Media in Higher Education."

7 "News Bits.," *NSTA Reports!* 27, no. 2 (September 2015): G3.

8 Eleni Mitsea and Athanasios Drigas, "A Journey into the Metacognitive Learning Strategies," *International Journal of Online and Biomedical Engineering (IJOE)* 15, no. 14 (October 26, 2019): 4–20.

9 Ibid.

10 Nielsen, Andersen, and Dau, "Podcast as a Learning Media in Higher Education."

11 Negretti and McGrath, "Scaffolding Genre Knowledge and Metacognition."

12 Prasanna Rathnayake, "Ascertaining Requisite Metacognitive Elements of Input through the Exploration of Language Learners' Cognitive Characteristics," *Sabaragamuwa University Journal* 16, no. 1 (September 10, 2018): 1, doi:10.4038/suslj.v16i1.7712.

13 Leigh A. Jones, "Podcasting and Performativity: Multimodal Invention in an Advanced Writing Class," n.d., 17.

14 Matthew Salesses, "'Pure Craft' Is a Lie," *Pleiades Magazine*, accessed February 13, 2022, https://pleiadesmag.com/pure-craft-is-a-lie-part-1/.

15 Mitsea and Drigas, "A Journey into the Metacognitive Learning Strategies."

16 Ibid.

17 Oualid Nemouchi, "Title: Metacognitive Strategies for EFL Writing," *Human Sciences Journal* 28, no. 48 (December 1, 2017): 159–74.

18 Jones, "Podcasting and Performativity: Multimodal Invention in an Advanced Writing Class."

19 Ibid., 86.

Chapter 4

1 Patricia M. Greenfield and Jean Lave, "Cognitive Aspects of Informal Education," *Cultural Perspectives on Child Development* 1 (1982): 192.

2 Michelle Salice Sugiyama, "Oral Storytelling as Evidence of Pedagogy in Forager Societies," *Frontier Psychology 8* (2017): 471.

3 George Lakoff and Mark Johnson, *Metaphors We Live By* (Chicago: University of Chicago Press, 2003).

4 Lambert, *Digital Storytelling.*

5 Andrew J. Bottomley, "Podcasting: A Decade in the Life of a 'New' Audio Medium: Introduction," *Journal of Radio & Audio Media* (Taylor & Francis, 2015).

6 James R. Alburger, *The Art of Voice Acting: The Craft and Business of Performing for Voice-Over*, 4th ed. (Burlington, MA: Focal Press, 2011).

7 Norm Sherman, "Drabbleclassics 25—Charlie the Purple Giraffe Was Acting Strangely (113)—The Drabblecast," *The Drabblecast*, accessed February 13, 2022, https://www.drabblecast.org/2015/11/09/drabbleclassics-25-charlie-the-purple-giraffe-was-acting-strangely-113/.

8 Todd Cochrane, *Podcasting: The Do-It-Yourself Guide*, ExtremeTech (Indianapolis, IN: Wiley Pub, 2005), 147–94.

9 Arlene Archer, "Power, Social Justice and Multimodal Pedagogies," *The Routledge Handbook of Multimodal Analysis* 2 (2014): 189–97; Marshall McLuhan, *Understanding Media: The Extensions of Man*, 1st MIT Press ed. (Cambridge, MA: MIT Press, 1994); bell hooks, *Teaching to Transgress: Education as the Practice of Freedom* (New York: Routledge, 1994); Gholnecsar "Gholdy" Muhammad and Lee Gonzalez, "Slam Poetry: An Artistic Resistance toward Identity, Agency, and Activism," *Equity & Excellence in Education* 49, no. 4 (2016): 440–53; Martha C. Pennington, "Literacy, Culture, and Creativity in a Digital Era," *Pedagogy: Critical Approaches to Teaching Literature, Language, Composition, and Culture* 17, no. 2 (2017): 259–87.

10 Muhammad and Gonzalez, "Slam Poetry."

Chapter 5

1 Martha C. Pennington, "'Literacy, Culture, and Creativity in a Digital Era," *Pedagogy* 17, no. 2 (2017): 280.

2 Steve Healey, "Beyond the Literary: Why Creative Literacy Matters," in *Key Issues in Creative Writing*, ed. Dianne Donnelly and Graeme Harper (Bristol: Multilingual Matters, 2013), 61–78.

3 Pennington, "Literacy, Culture, and Creativity in a Digital Era," 262.

4 Felicia Rose Chavez, *The Anti-Racist Writing Workshop: How to Decolonize the Creative Classroom* (Chicago: Haymarket Books, 2021), 8.

5 Pennington, "Literacy, Culture, and Creativity in a Digital Era," 261.

6 Ibid., 266.

7 Ibid., 259.

8 Ibid., 263.

9 Ibid.

10 Ibid., 264.

11 Chavez, *The Anti-Racist Writing Workshop*, 3.

12 Healey, "Beyond the Literary," 61.

13 Ibid., 62.

14 Ibid.

15 Ibid., 63.

16 Pennington, "Literacy, Culture, and Creativity in a Digital Era," 268.

17 Ibid., 271.

18 Ibid., 268.

19 Lavanya Ramanathan, "From Instapoets to the Bards of YouTube, Poetry Is Going Viral. And Some Poets Hate That," *The Washington Post* 6 (2018). https://www.washingtonpost.com/lifestyle/style/from-instapoets-to-the-bards-of-youtube-poetry-is-going-viral-and-some-poets-hate-that/2018/05/06/ea4240fa-4329-11e8-8569-26fda6b404c7_story.html.

20 Chavez, *The Anti-Racist Writing Workshop*, 3.

21 Ibid., 99–100.

22 Edward Hirsch, "How to Read a Poem | Academy of American Poets," *Poets.org*, accessed November 26, 2007, https://poets.org/text/how-read-poem-0.

23 Ibid.

24 Tracy K. Smith, "303: Telling My Father," *The Slowdown*, hosted by Tracy K. Smith, accessed October 17, 2021, https://www.slowdownshow.org/episode/2020/01/22/303-telling-my-father.

25 Ibid.

26 James Crews, "Telling My Father," *The Slowdown*, l. 9, accessed February 13, 2022, https://www.slowdownshow.org/episode/2020/01/22/303-telling-my-father.

27 Ibid., ll. 11–14.

28 Ibid., ll. 15–19.

29 Arthur W. Frank, "'Who's There?': A Vulnerable Reading of *Hamlet*," *Literature and Medicine* 37, no. 2 (2019): 396–419.

30 Pennington, "Literacy, Culture, and Creativity in a Digital Era," 279.

31 David Bell, "The University in Your Pocket," in *Podcasting for Learning in Universities*, ed. Gilly Salmon and Palitha Edirisingha (Maidenhead: McGraw-Hill International (UK) Ltd., 2008), 179.

32 Dianne Forbes, "Beyond Lecture Capture: Student-Generated Podcasts in Teacher Education," *Waikato Journal of Education* 16, no. 1 (May 31, 2011): 53, doi:10.15663/wje.v16i1.70.

33 Ibid., 42.

34 Ibid., 53.

35 Chris Cane and Annette Cashmore, "Students' Podcasts as Learning Tools," *Podcasting for Learning in Universities*, ed. Gilly Salmon and Palitha Edirisingha (Maidenhead: McGraw-Hill International (UK) Ltd., 2008), 147.

36 Ibid., 148.

37 Matthew Salesses, *Craft in the Real World: Rethinking Fiction Writing and Workshopping* (New York: Catapult, 2021), 32.

38 Ibid., 14.

39 Healey, "Beyond the Literary," 75.

40 Ibid.

41 Ibid.

42 Ibid.

43 Palitha Edirisingha, Gilly Salmon, and Ming Nie, "Developing Pedagogical Podcasts," in *Podcasting for Learning in Universities*, ed. Gilly Salmon and Palitha Edirisingha (Maidenhead: McGraw-Hill Education (UK), 2008), 154.

44 Ibid., 155.

45 Tracey Costley, Alice Chik, and Martha C. Pennington, "Towards a Creativity and Discovery-Based University Writing Curriculum," in *Creativity and Discovery in the University Writing Class: A Teacher's Guide*, ed. Tracey Costley, Alice Chik, and Martha C. Pennington (Bristol, CT: Equinox Publishing, 2015), 2–3.

46 Forbes, "Beyond Lecture Capture," 54–5.

47 Chavez, *The Anti-Racist Writing Workshop*, 31.

48 Smith, "303"; Tracy K. Smith, "320: How Can Black People Write About Flowers at a Time Like This," *The Slowdown*, accessed October 17, 2021, https://www.slowdownshow.org/episode/2020/02/14/320-how-can-black-people-write-about-flowers-at-a-time-like-this.

49 Elizabeth Bishop, "One Art by Elizabeth Bishop | Poetry Foundation," *Poetry Foundation*, 2021, https://www.poetryfoundation.org/poems/47536/one-art; Wesli Court, "The Obsession," *Poetics and Ruminations*, accessed April 4, 2010, https://lewisturco.typepad.com/poetics/2010/04/the-obsession.html; Kim Addonizio, "Stolen Moments," text/html, *Poetry Foundation* (Poetry Magazine, 2021), https://www.poetryfoundation.org/, https://www.poetryfoundation.org/poetrymagazine/poems/40660/stolen-moments.

50 Tupac Amaru Shakur, *The Rose That Grew from Concrete* (London: MTV Books, 2009); Rupi Kaur, *Milk and Honey* (Kansas City, MO: Andrews McMeel Publishing, 2015); Linda Ellis, "The Dash," in *The Dash: Making a Difference with Your Life*, ed. Linda Ellis and Mac Anderson (Nashville, TN: Thomas Nelson, Inc, 2012), 6–23.

51 Healey, "Beyond the Literary," 68.

52 Ibid.

53 Chavez, *The Anti-Racist Writing Workshop*, 9.

54 Chavez, *The Anti-Racist Writing Workshop*.

55 Ibid., 40.

56 Hirsch, "How to Read a Poem | Academy of American Poets."

57 Edirisingha, Salmon, and Nie, "Developing Pedagogical Podcasts," 164.

58 Ibid.

59 Ibid., 153.

60 Cathryn Molloy et al., "A Dialogue on Possibilities for Embodied Methodologies in the Rhetoric of Health & Medicine," *Rhetoric of Health & Medicine* 1, no. 3 (2018): 367.

61 Edirisingha, Salmon, and Nie, "Developing Pedagogical Podcasts," 154.

62 Forbes, "Beyond Lecture Capture," 54.

63 Gilly Salmon, "The Future for Podcasting," in *Podcasting for Learning in Universities*, ed. Gilly Salmon and Palitha Edirisingha (Maidenhead: McGraw-Hill Education (UK), 2008), 172.

64 Ibid.

65 Chavez, *The Anti-Racist Writing Workshop*, 23.

66 Martha C. Pennington, "Towards a Creative Writing Pedagogy," *Writing and Pedagogy* 4, no. 2 (2012): 156.

Chapter 6

1 Anna Leahy and et al., "Theories of Creativity and Creative Writing Pedagogy," in *The Handbook of Creative Writing*, ed. Steven Earnshaw, Second edition (Edinburgh: Edinburgh University Press, 2014), 12.

2 Ibid., 18.

3 Ibid., 14.

4 Nguyen, "Unsilencing the Writing Workshop ‹ Literary Hub."

5 Ibid.

6 Ibid.

7 Ibid.

8 Díaz, "MFA *vs*. POC."

9 Ibid.

10 Chavez, *The Anti-Racist Writing Workshop*, 3.

11 Roxane Gay, "Where Things Stand," *The Rumpus*, June 7, 2012, https://therumpus.net/2012/06/where-things-stand/.

12 Chavez, *The Anti-Racist Writing Workshop*, 9.

13 Ibid.

14 Nguyen, "Unsilencing the Writing Workshop ‹ Literary Hub."

15 Ibid.

16 Brenda Miller and Suzanne Paola, *Tell It Slant: Creating, Refining, and Publishing Creative Nonfiction*, Third edition (New York: McGraw Hill, 2019), 127–30.

17 qtd. in Vivian Gornick, *The Situation and the Story: The Art of Personal Narrative*, New edition for writers, teachers, and students, 1st pbk. ed. (New York: Farrar, Straus, and Giroux, 2002), 91.

18 Jenny Spinner, Kate Dobson, and Lynn Z. Bloom, "Creating Nonfiction Writers: A Dialogue," *Writing on the Edge* 26, no. 2 (2016): 31.

19 Ibid.

20 Ibid., 24.

21 Ibid.

22 Miller and Paola, *Tell It Slant*, 9.

23 qtd. in ibid., 4–5.

24 Spinner, Dobson, and Bloom, "Creating Nonfiction Writers," 26.

25 Dylan Landis, "Going Cold: Writing Emotion, the Earley Scale, and the Brilliance of Edwidge Danticat," *Brevity: A Journal of Concise Literary Nonfiction*, accessed February 12, 2022, https://brevitymag.com/craft-essays/going-cold/.

26 Ibid.

27 Ibid.

28 Sean Prentiss and Jessica Hendry Nelson, *Advanced Creative Nonfiction: A Writer's and Illustrator's Guide and Anthology*, Bloomsbury Writers' Guides and Anthologies (London and New York: Bloomsbury Academic, 2021), 15.

29 Ibid.

30 Czesław Miłosz and Catherine S. Leach, *Native Realm: A Search for Self-Definition* (New York: Farrar, Straus and Giroux, 2002), 20.

Chapter 7

1 Kase Johnstun, *LITerally Ep. 42—Sunni Wilkinson*, LITerally (The Banyon Collective, 2020), https://www.youtube.com/watch?v=ym07vMiM8eo.

Chapter 8

1 Umberto Eco, *Six Walks in the Fictional Woods* (Cambridge, MA: Harvard University Press, 1998).

2 Lisa Ede and Andrea Lunsford, "Audience Addressed/Audience Invoked: The Role of Audience in Composition Theory and Pedagogy," *College Composition and Communication* 35, no. 2 (May 1984): 155, doi:10.2307/358093.

3 Jack Selzer, "More Meanings of Audience," in *A Rhetoric of Doing: Essays on Written Discourse in Honor of James L. Kinneavy*, ed. James L. Kinneavy et al. (Southern Illinois UP Carbondale, 1992), 161–77.

4 Ibid., 166.

5 Eco, *Six Walks in the Fictional Woods.*

6 Ede and Lunsford, "Audience Addressed/Audience Invoked," 168.

7 John Moe, *The Hilarious World of Depression*, accessed December 10, 2022, https://www.hilariousworld.org/episodes.

8 Ibid.

9 Ibid.

10 Laith Zuraikat, "The Parasocial Nature of the Podcast," in *Radio's Second Century: Past, Present, and Future Perspectives*, ed. John Allen Hendricks (New Brunswick, NJ: Rutgers University Press, 2020), 39–52.

11 Berry, "Will the iPod Kill the Radio Star?"

12 Anna Jaakonaho, "Intimate Listening: Exploring Audience's Podcast Experiences through the Case of Ångestpodden" (Lund University, 2021), https://lup.lub.lu.se/luur/download?func=downloadFile&recordOId=9044320&fileOId=9054844.

13 Zuraikat, "The Parasocial Nature of the Podcast."

14 Shannon Bond, "What the Joe Rogan Podcast Controversy Says about the Online Misinformation Ecosystem," *NPR*, January 21, 2022, sec. Arts & Life, https://www.npr.org/2022/01/21/1074442185/joe-rogan-doctor-covid-podcast-spotify-misinformation.

15 Ede and Lunsford, "Audience Addressed/Audience Invoked."

16 Lydia French and Emily Bloom, "Auralacy: From Plato to Podcasting and Back Again," *Currents in Electronic Literacy*, 2011.

17 Ibid.

18 Palmeri, *Remixing Composition.*

19 Ibid.

20 Qtd. in Dario llinares, Neil Fox, and Richard Berry, eds., *Podcasting: New Aural Cultures and Digital Media*, 1st ed. (New York: Springer Science+Business Media, LLC, 2018).

21 Jason Earle, "Teachers and Popular Culture Consumption: Notes toward an Alternative Theory of Teachers' Non-Appropriation of Instructional Research," *Popular Culture and Critical Pedagogy: Reading, Constructing, Connecting*, 2000, 122.

22 Ibid.

23 Ibid.

24 Ibid., 123.

Chapter 9

1 Benjamin Herold, "Schools Handed Out Millions of Digital Devices Under COVID-19. Now, Thousands Are Missing," *Education Week*, July 24, 2020, sec. IT Infrastructure, https://www.edweek.org/technology/schools-handed-out-millions-of-digital-devices-under-covid-19-now-thousands-are-missing/2020/07; Erin Richards Mansfield Elinor Aspegren and Erin, "A Year into the Pandemic, Thousands of Students Still Can't Get Reliable WiFi for School. The Digital Divide Remains Worse than Ever.," *USA TODAY*, accessed January 30, 2022, https://www.usatoday.com/story/news/education/2021/02/04/covid-online-school-broadband-internet-laptops/3930744001/; Colleen Mcclain et al., "The Internet and the Pandemic," *Pew Research Center: Internet, Science & Tech*, September 1, 2021, https://www.pewresearch.org/internet/2021/09/01/the-internet-and-the-pandemic/; Palm Beach County Board of Education, "Policy 8.124—School District of Palm Beach County 2 Electronic Device Take Home Policy" (Palm Beach County, 2021), https://bocanewsnow.com/wp-content/uploads/2021/02/PBSD-devices.pdf.

2 Palm Beach County Board of Education, "Policy 8.124—School District of Palm Beach County 2 Electronic Device Take Home Policy."

3 Ibid.

4 Mcclain et al., "The Internet and the Pandemic."

5 "More than 9 Million Children Lack Internet Access at Home for Online Learning," *USAFacts*, October 19, 2020, https://usafacts.org/articles/internet-access-students-at-home/.

6 Mcclain et al., "The Internet and the Pandemic."

7 Dana Goldstein, Adam Popescu, and Nikole Hannah-Jones, "As School Moves Online, Many Students Stay Logged Out," *The New York Times*, April 6, 2020, sec. U.S., https://www.nytimes.com/2020/04/06/us/coronavirus-schools-attendance-absent.html.

8 Ibid.

9 Andrew Perrin, "Mobile Technology and Home Broadband 2021," *Pew Research Center: Internet, Science & Tech*, June 3, 2021, https://www.pewresearch.org/internet/2021/06/03/mobile-technology-and-home-broadband-2021/; Andrew Perrin and Sara Atske, "Americans with Disabilities Less Likely than Those without to Own Some Digital Devices," *Pew Research Center*, accessed January 31, 2022, https://www.pewresearch.org/fact-tank/2021/09/10/americans-with-disabilities-less-likely-than-those-without-to-own-some-digital-devices/; Sara Atske and Andrew Perrin, "Home Broadband Adoption, Computer Ownership Vary by Race, Ethnicity in the U.S.," *Pew Research Center*, accessed January 31, 2022, https://www.pewresearch.org/fact-tank/2021/07/16/home-broadband-adoption-computer-ownership-vary-by-race-ethnicity-in-the-u-s/.

10 Barbara Jean Monroe, *Crossing the Digital Divide: Race, Writing, and Technology in the Classroom*, Language and Literacy Series (New York: Teachers College Press, 2004).

11 Tisha Lewis Ellison and Marva Solomon, "Counter-Storytelling *vs.* Deficit Thinking around African American Children and Families, Digital Literacies, Race, and the Digital Divide," *Research in the Teaching of English* 53, no. 3 (2019): 223.

12 Ibid.

13 Lee, "Spotify Ramps up Podcast Deals with Influencers"; Photini Vrikki and Sarita Malik, "Voicing Lived-Experience and Anti-Racism: Podcasting as a Space at the Margins for Subaltern Counterpublics," *Popular Communication* 17, no. 4 (October 2, 2019): 273–87, doi:10.1080/15405702.2019.1622116.

14 "First-Ever Black Podcast Listener Report Finds Big Growth in Reach," *insideradio.com*, accessed February 9, 2022, http://www.insideradio.com/free/first-ever-black-podcast-listener-report-finds-big-growth-in-reach/article_e5c9a3a4-3e04-11ec-840b-a78ee1ea854c.html.

15 Vrikki and Malik, "Voicing Lived-Experience and Anti-Racism."

16 "First-Ever Black Podcast Listener Report Finds Big Growth in Reach."

Afterword

1 Nielsen, Andersen, and Dau, "Podcast as a Learning Media in Higher Education," 424.

2 Marissa DeCuir, "Why Audiobooks Are Skyrocketing, and How Writers Can Take Advantage in 2022," *Writer's Digest*, accessed May 11, 2022, https://www.writersdigest.com/getting-published/why-audiobooks-are-skyrocketing-and-how-writers-can-take-advantage-in-2022.

Bibliography

Addonizio, Kim. "Stolen Moments." Text/html. *Poetry Foundation*. Poetry Magazine, 2021. https://www.poetryfoundation.org/, https://www.poetryfoundation.org/poetrymagazine/poems/40660/stolen-moments.

Aitken, Hugh G. J. "Allocating the Spectrum: The Origins of Radio Regulation." *Technology and Culture* 35, no. 4 (October 1994): 686. doi:10.2307/3106503.

Alburger, James R. *The Art of Voice Acting: The Craft and Business of Performing for Voice-Over*. 4th ed. Burlington, MA: Focal Press, 2011.

Archer, Arlene. "Power, Social Justice and Multimodal Pedagogies." *The Routledge Handbook of Multimodal Analysis* 2 (2014): 189–97.

Atske, Sara and Andrew Perrin. "Home Broadband Adoption, Computer Ownership Vary by Race, Ethnicity in the U.S." *Pew Research Center*. Accessed January 31, 2022. https://www.pewresearch.org/fact-tank/2021/07/16/home-broadband-adoption-computer-ownership-vary-by-race-ethnicity-in-the-u-s/.

Bell, David. "The University in Your Pocket." In *Podcasting for Learning in Universities*, ed. Gilly Salmon and Palitha Edirisingha, 178–87. Maidenhead: McGraw-Hill International (UK) Ltd., 2008. http://public.eblib.com/choice/publicfullrecord.aspx?p=369506.

Bishop, Elizabeth. "One Art by Elizabeth Bishop | Poetry Foundation." *Poetry Foundation*, 2021. https://www.poetryfoundation.org/poems/47536/one-art.

Black, David A. "Internet Radio: A Case Study in Medium Specificity." *Media, Culture & Society* 23, no. 3 (2001): 397–408.

Bond, Shannon. "What the Joe Rogan Podcast Controversy Says about the Online Misinformation Ecosystem." *NPR*, January 21, 2022, sec. Arts & Life. https://www.npr.org/2022/01/21/1074442185/joe-rogan-doctor-covid-podcast-spotify-misinformation.

Bonini, Tiziano. "The 'Second Age' of Podcasting: Reframing Podcasting as a New Digital Mass Medium." *Quaderns Del CAC* 41, no. 18 (2015): 21–30.

Botticello, Julie. "Engaging Many Voices for Inclusivity in Higher Education," May 26, 2020. doi:10.15123/uel.8805x.

Bottomley, Andrew J. "Podcasting: A Decade in the Life of a 'New' Audio Medium: Introduction." *Journal of Radio & Audio Media*. Taylor & Francis, 2015.

Bridge, Gavin. "Netflix Released More Originals Than the Whole TV Industry Did in 2005." *Variety*, December 17, 2019. https://variety.com/2019/tv/news/netflix-more-2019-originals-than-entire-tv-industry-in-2005-1203441709/.

Buckley, Francis J. *Team Teaching: What, Why, and How?* Thousand Oaks, CA: SAGE Publications, Inc, 2000. https://search.ebscohost.com/login.aspx?direct=true&db=nlebk&AN=474657&site=eds-live.

Cane, Chris and Annette Cashmore. "Students' Podcasts as Learning Tools." *Podcasting for Learning in Universities*, 2008, 146–52.

Chavez, Felicia Rose. *The Anti-Racist Writing Workshop: Decolonizing the Creative Classroom*. Chicago: Haymarket Books, 2021.

Cochrane, Todd. *Podcasting: The Do-It-Yourself Guide*. ExtremeTech. Indianapolis, IN: Wiley Pub, 2005.

Costley, Tracey, Alice Chik, and Martha C. Pennington. "Towards a Creativity and Discovery-Based University Writing Curriculum." In *Creativity and Discovery in the University Writing Class: A Teacher's Guide*, ed. Alice Chik, Tracey Costley, and Martha C. Pennington, 2–3. Equinox Publishing, 2015.

Court, Wesli. "The Obsession." *Poetics and Ruminations*, April 4, 2010. https://lewisturco.typepad.com/poetics/2010/04/the-obsession.html.

Crews, James. "Telling My Father." *The Slowdown*. Accessed February 13, 2022. https://www.slowdownshow.org/episode/2020/01/22/303-telling-my-father.

Davis, Leslie and Richard Fry. "College Faculty Still Far Less Diverse than Students in Race, Ethnicity | Pew Research Center." *Pew Research Center*, July 31, 2019. https://www.pewresearch.org/fact-tank/2019/07/31/us-college-faculty-student-diversity/.

DeCuir, Marissa. "Why Audiobooks Are Skyrocketing, and How Writers Can Take Advantage in 2022." *Writer's Digest*. Accessed May 11, 2022. https://www.writersdigest.com/getting-published/why-audiobooks-are-skyrocketing-and-how-writers-can-take-advantage-in-2022.

Díaz, Junot. "MFA *vs.* POC." *The New Yorker*, April 30, 2014. https://www.newyorker.com/books/page-turner/mfa-vs-poc.

Earle, Jason. "Teachers and Popular Culture Consumption: Notes toward an Alternative Theory of Teachers' Non-Appropriation of Instructional Research." *Popular Culture and Critical Pedagogy: Reading, Constructing, Connecting*, 2000, 122.

Eco, Umberto. *Six Walks in the Fictional Woods*. Cambridge, MA: Harvard University Press, 1998.

Ede, Lisa and Andrea Lunsford. "Audience Addressed/Audience Invoked: The Role of Audience in Composition Theory and Pedagogy." *College Composition and Communication* 35, no. 2 (May 1984): 155. doi:10.2307/358093.

Edirisingha, Palitha, Gilly Salmon, and Ming Nie. "Developing Pedagogical Podcasts." In *Podcasting for Learning in Universities*, ed. Gilly Salmon and Palitha Edirisingha, 154. McGraw-Hill Education (UK), 2008.

Elbow, Peter. "Reading Out Loud to Improve Writing." *Peter Elbow: The Democratization of Writing*. Accessed December 10, 2021. https://peterelbow.com/handouts.html.

Elbow, Peter. "What Do We Mean When We Talk about Voice in Texts?" *Voices on Voice: Perspectives, Definitions, Inquiry*, January 1, 1994, 1–35.

Ellis, Linda. "The Dash." In *The Dash: Making a Difference with Your Life*, ed. Linda Ellis and Mac Anderson, 6–23. Champaign Il: Thomas Nelson, Inc, 2005.

Ellison, Tisha Lewis and Marva Solomon. "Counter-Storytelling *vs.* Deficit Thinking around African American Children and Families, Digital Literacies, Race, and the Digital Divide." *Research in the Teaching of English* 53, no. 3 (2019): 23.

Forbes, Dianne. "Beyond Lecture Capture: Student-Generated Podcasts in Teacher Education." *Waikato Journal of Education* 16, no. 1 (May 31, 2011). doi:10.15663/wje.v16i1.70.

Frank, Arthur W. "'Who's There?': A Vulnerable Reading of *Hamlet*." *Literature and Medicine* 37, no. 2 (2019): 396–419.

French, Lydia and Emily Bloom. "Auralacy: From Plato to Podcasting and Back Again." *Currents in Electronic Literacy*, 2011.

Friedman, Batya and Helen Nissenbaum. "Bias in Computer Systems." *ACM Transactions on Information Systems (TOIS)* 14, no. 3 (1996): 330–47.

Gay, Roxane. "Where Things Stand." *The Rumpus*, June 7, 2012. https://therumpus.net/2012/06/where-things-stand/.

Goldstein, Dana, Adam Popescu, and Nikole Hannah-Jones. "As School Moves Online, Many Students Stay Logged Out." *The New York Times*, April 6, 2020, sec. U.S. https://www.nytimes.com/2020/04/06/us/coronavirus-schools-attendance-absent.html.

Gornick, Vivian. *The Situation and the Story: The Art of Personal Narrative*. New ed. for writers, Teachers, and Students, 1st pbk. ed. New York: Farrar, Straus, and Giroux, 2002.

Greenfield, Patricia M. and Jean Lave. "Cognitive Aspects of Informal Education." *Cultural Perspectives on Child Development* 1 (1982): 181–207.

Han, Jimin. "Jimin Han on Rethinking the CW Workshop." *Pleiades Magazine*, 2015. https://pleiadesmag.com/jimin-han-on-rethinking-the-cw-workshop/.

Have, Iben and Birgitte Stougaard Pedersen. "Reading Audiobooks." In *Beyond Media Borders, Volume 1: Intermedial Relations among Multimodal Media*, ed. Lars Elleström. Cham: Springer International Publishing, 2021. doi:10.1007/978-3-030-49679-1.

Healey, Steve. "Beyond the Literary: Why Creative Literacy Matters." In *Key Issues in Creative Writing*, ed. Dianne Donnelly and Graeme Harper, 61–78. Bristol: Multilingual Matters, 2013.

Herold, Benjamin. "Schools Handed Out Millions of Digital Devices Under COVID-19. Now, Thousands Are Missing." *Education Week*, July 24, 2020, sec. IT Infrastructure. https://www.edweek.org/technology/schools-handed-out-millions-of-digital-devices-under-covid-19-now-thousands-are-missing/2020/07.

Hirsch, Edward. "How to Read a Poem | Academy of American Poets." *Poets.Org*, November 26, 2007. https://poets.org/text/how-read-poem-0.

Hoeft, Mary E. "Why University Students Don't Read: What Professors Can Do To Increase Compliance." *International Journal for the Scholarship of Teaching and Learning* 6, no. 2 (July 1, 2012). doi:10.20429/ijsotl.2012.060212.

Honig, David. "How the FCC Suppressed Minority Broadcast Ownership and How the FCC Can Undo the Damage It Caused." *S. Region Black Students Ass'n LJ* 12 (2018): 44.

hooks, bell. *Teaching to Transgress: Education as the Practice of Freedom*. New York: Routledge, 1994.

"Hooper Ratings Summer, 1947." C.E. Hooper Inc., 1947. https://worldradiohistory.com/Archive-Ratings/Hooperratings-Summer-1947.pdf.

insideradio.com. "First-Ever Black Podcast Listener Report Finds Big Growth In Reach." Accessed February 9, 2022. http://www.insideradio.com/free/first-ever-black-podcast

-listener-report-finds-big-growth-in-reach/article_e5c9a3a4-3e04-11ec-840b-a78ee1ea854c.html.

Jaakonaho, Anna. "Intimate Listening: Exploring Audience's Podcast Experiences through the Case of Ångestpodden." Lund University, 2021. https://lup.lub.lu.se/luur/download?func=downloadFile&recordOId=9044320&fileOId=9054844.

Jewitt, Carey. "Multimodality and Literacy in School Classrooms." *Review of Research in Education* 32, no. 1 (February 2008): 241–67. doi:10.3102/0091732X07310586.

Johnson, David W., Roger T. Johnson, and Karl A. Smith. *Cooperative Learning: Increasing College Faculty Instructional Productivity*. ASHE-ERIC Higher Education Report, no. 4, 1991. Washington, DC: School of Education and Human Development, George Washington University, 1991.

Johnstun, Kase. *LITerally Ep. 42—Sunni Wilkinson*. LITerally. The Banyan Collective, 2020. https://www.youtube.com/watch?v=ym07vMiM8eo.

Jones, Leigh A. "Podcasting and Performativity: Multimodal Invention in an Advanced Writing Class." n.d., 17.

Kaur, Rupi. *Milk and Honey*. Kansas City, MO: Andrews McMeel Publishing, 2015.

Keen, Suzanne. "A Theory of Narrative Empathy." *Narrative* 14, no. 3 (2006): 207–36.

Lakoff, George and Mark Johnson. *Metaphors We Live By*. Chicago: University of Chicago Press, 2003.

Lambert, Joe. *Digital Storytelling: Capturing Lives, Creating Community*. 4th ed. New York and London: Routledge, 2013.

Landis, Dylan. "Going Cold: Writing Emotion, the Earley Scale, and the Brilliance of Edwidge Danticat." *Brevity: A Journal of Concise Literary Nonfiction*. Accessed February 12, 2022. https://brevitymag.com/craft-essays/going-cold/.

Leahy, Anna et al. "Theories of Creativity and Creative Writing Pedagogy." In *The Handbook of Creative Writing*, ed. Steven Earnshaw, 2nd ed., 11–23. Edinburgh: Edinburgh University Press, 2014.

Lee, Wendy. "Spotify Ramps up Podcast Deals with Influencers." *Los Angeles Times*, August 27, 2020. https://www.latimes.com/entertainment-arts/business/story/2020-08-27/spotify-podcast-deals-influencers.

Levi, Lili. "The Four Eras of FCC Public Interest Regulation." *Administrative Law Review* 60 (2008): 813.

Lindgren, Mia. "Personal Narrative Journalism and Podcasting." *Radio Journal: International Studies in Broadcast & Audio Media* 14, no. 1 (2016): 23–41.

Llinares, Dario, Neil Fox, and Richard Berry, eds. *Podcasting: New Aural Cultures and Digital Media*. 1st ed. New York: Springer Science+Business Media, LLC, 2018.

Mcclain, Colleen, Emily A Vogels, Andrew Perrin, Stella Sechopoulos, and Lee Rainie. "The Internet and the Pandemic." *Pew Research Center: Internet, Science & Tech*, September 1, 2021. https://www.pewresearch.org/internet/2021/09/01/the-internet-and-the-pandemic/.

McGurl, Mark. *The Program Era: Postwar Fiction and the Rise of Creative Writing*. 1st Harvard University Press pbk ed. Cambridge, MA: Harvard University Press, 2011.

McLuhan, Marshall. *Understanding Media: The Extensions of Man*. 1st MIT Press ed. Cambridge, MA: MIT Press, 1994.

Menand, Louis. "Show or Tell." *The New Yorker*. Accessed October 4, 2020. https://www.newyorker.com/magazine/2009/06/08/show-or-tell.

Miller, Brenda and Suzanne Paola. *Tell It Slant: Creating, Refining, and Publishing Creative Nonfiction*. 3rd ed. New York: McGraw Hill, 2019.

Miller, Carolyn Handler. *Digital Storytelling: A Creator's Guide to Interactive Entertainment*. 3rd ed. New York: Focal Press, Taylor & Francis Group, 2014.

Miłosz, Czesław and Catherine S. Leach. *Native Realm: A Search for Self-Definition*. New York: Farrar, Straus and Giroux, 2002.

Mitsea, Eleni and Athanasios Drigas. "A Journey into the Metacognitive Learning Strategies." *International Journal of Online and Biomedical Engineering (IJOE)* 15, no. 14 (October 26, 2019): 4–20.

Moe, John. *The Hilarious World of Depression*. Accessed December 10, 2022. https://www.hilariousworld.org/episodes.

Molloy, Cathryn, Cristy Beemer, Jeffrey Bennett, Ann Green, Jenell Johnson, Molly Kessler, Maria Novotny, and Bryna Siegel-Finer. "A Dialogue on Possibilities for Embodied Methodologies in the Rhetoric of Health & Medicine." *Rhetoric of Health & Medicine* 1, no. 3 (2018): 349–71.

Monroe, Barbara Jean. *Crossing the Digital Divide: Race, Writing, and Technology in the Classroom*. Language and Literacy Series. New York: Teachers College Press, 2004.

Muhammad, Gholnecsar "Gholdy" and Lee Gonzalez. "Slam Poetry: An Artistic Resistance toward Identity, Agency, and Activism." *Equity & Excellence in Education* 49, no. 4 (2016): 440–53.

Negretti, Raffaella and Lisa McGrath. "Scaffolding Genre Knowledge and Metacognition: Insights from an L2 Doctoral Research Writing Course." *Journal of Second Language Writing* 40 (June 2018): 12–31. doi:10.1016/j.jslw.2017.12.002.

Nelson, Craig E. "Every Course Differently: Diversity and College Teaching: An Outline." *National Science Foundation Publication*, 1993, 93–108.

Nemouchi, Oualid. "Metacognitive Strategies for EFL Writing." مجلة العلوم الإنسانية, no. 48 (December 1, 2017): 159–74.

"News Bits." *NSTA Reports!* 27, no. 2 (September 2015): G3.

Nguyen, Beth. "Unsilencing the Writing Workshop ‹ Literary Hub." *LitHub*, April 3, 2019. https://lithub.com/unsilencing-the-writing-workshop/.

Nielsen, Stine Nørkjær, René Holm Andersen, and Susanne Dau. "Podcast as a Learning Media in Higher Education." In *Proceedings of the European Conference on E-Learning*, 424, 2018.

NPR.org. "NPR Podcasts & Shows." Accessed February 12, 2022 https://www.npr.org/podcasts-and-shows/.

Palm Beach County Board of Education. "Policy 8.124—School District of Palm Beach County 2 Electronic Device Take Home Policy." Palm Beach County, 2021. https://bocanewsnow.com/wp-content/uploads/2021/02/PBSD-devices.pdf.

Palmeri, Jason. *Remixing Composition: A History of Multimodal Writing Pedagogy*. Carbondale and Edwardsville: SIU Press, 2012.

Park, Taeyeol. "Engaging Students through a Podcast Assignment in Canvas LMS." *Association for the Advancement of Computing in Education (AACE)*, 1101–3. 2019. https://www.learntechlib.org/primary/p/207782/.

Pennington, Martha C. "Literacy, Culture, and Creativity in a Digital Era." *Pedagogy: Critical Approaches to Teaching Literature, Language, Composition, and Culture* 17, no. 2 (2017): 259–87.

Pennington, Martha C. "Towards a Creative Writing Pedagogy." *Writing and Pedagogy* 4, no. 2 (2012): 151–8.

Perez, Sarah. "Spotify Says US Podcast Listeners Now Use Its Service More than Apple Podcasts | TechCrunch." *TechCrunch*, October 27, 2021. https://techcrunch.com/2021/10/27/spotify-says-u-s-podcast-listeners-now-use-its-service-more-than-apple-podcasts/.

Perrin, Andrew. "Mobile Technology and Home Broadband 2021." *Pew Research Center: Internet, Science & Tech*, June 3, 2021. https://www.pewresearch.org/internet/2021/06/03/mobile-technology-and-home-broadband-2021/.

Perrin, Andrew and Sara Atske. "Americans with Disabilities Less Likely than Those without to Own Some Digital Devices." *Pew Research Center*. Accessed January 31, 2022. https://www.pewresearch.org/fact-tank/2021/09/10/americans-with-disabilities-less-likely-than-those-without-to-own-some-digital-devices/.

Prentiss, Sean and Jessica Hendry Nelson. *Advanced Creative Nonfiction: A Writer's and Illustrator's Guide and Anthology*. Bloomsbury Writers' Guides and Anthologies. London and New York: Bloomsbury Academic, 2021.

Ramanathan, Lavanya. "From Instapoets to the Bards of YouTube, Poetry Is Going Viral. And Some Poets Hate That." *The Washington Post* 6 (2018). https://www.washingtonpost.com/lifestyle/style/from-instapoets-to-the-bards-of-youtube-poetry-is-going-viral-and-some-poets-hate-that/2018/05/06/ea4240fa-4329-11e8-8569-26fda6b404c7_story.html.

Rathnayake, Prasanna. "Ascertaining Requisite Metacognitive Elements of Input through the Exploration of Language Learners' Cognitive Characteristics." *Sabaragamuwa University Journal* 16, no. 1 (September 10, 2018): 1. doi:10.4038/suslj.v16i1.7712.

Richard, Berry. "Will the iPod Kill the Radio Star? Profiling Podcasting as Radio." *Convergence: The International Journal of Research into New Media Technologies* 12, no. 2 (May 2006): 143–62. doi:10.1177/1354856506066522.

Richards, Erin, Elinor Aspegren and Erin Mansfield. "A Year into the Pandemic, Thousands of Students Still Can't Get Reliable WiFi for School. The Digital Divide Remains Worse than Ever." *USA TODAY*. Accessed January 30, 2022. https://www.usatoday.com/story/news/education/2021/02/04/covid-online-school-broadband-internet-laptops/3930744001/.

Salesses, Matthew. *Craft in the Real World: Rethinking Fiction Writing and Workshopping*. New York: Catapult, 2021.

Salesses, Matthew. "'Pure Craft' Is a Lie." *Pleiades Magazine*. Accessed February 13, 2022. https://pleiadesmag.com/pure-craft-is-a-lie-part-1/.

Salesses, Matthew. "When Defending Your Writing Becomes Defending Yourself." *NPR*, July 20, 2014. https://www.npr.org/sections/codeswitch/2014/07/20/313158511/salesses-writers-workshop-diversity.

Salmon, Gilly. "The Future for Podcasting." In *Podcasting for Learning in Universities*, ed. Palitha Edirisingha and Gilly Salmon, 169–77. McGraw-Hill Education (UK), 2008.

ebookcentral-proquest-com.ezp.scranton.edu/lib/scranton-ebooks/detail.action?docID=369506.

Selzer, Jack. "More Meanings of Audience." In *A Rhetoric of Doing: Essays on Written Discourse in Honor of James L. Kinneavy*, ed. James L. Kinneavy et al., 161–77. Boston: Southern Illinois UP Carbondale, 1992.

Shakur, Tupac Amaru. *The Rose That Grew from Concrete*. London: MTV Books, 2009.

Sherman, Norm. "Drabbleclassics 25—Charlie the Purple Giraffe Was Acting Strangely (113)—The Drabblecast." *The Drabblecast*. Accessed February 13, 2022. https://www.drabblecast.org/2015/11/09/drabbleclassics-25-charlie-the-purple-giraffe-was-acting-strangely-113/.

Smith, Tracy K. "303: Telling My Father." *The Slowdown*, hosted by Tracy K. Smith. Accessed October 17, 2021. https://www.slowdownshow.org/episode/2020/01/22/303-telling-my-father.

Smith, Tracy K. "320: How Can Black People Write About Flowers at a Time Like This." *The Slowdown*. Accessed October 17, 2021. https://www.slowdownshow.org/episode/2020/02/14/320-how-can-black-people-write-about-flowers-at-a-time-like-this.

Spangler, Todd. "Netflix's Amortized Content Spending to Rise 26% to $13.6 Billion in 2021, Analysts Project." *Variety*, September 2021. https://www.yahoo.com/now/netflix-amortized-content-spending-rise-184211094.html.

Spinner, Jenny, Kate Dobson, and Lynn Z Bloom. "Creating Nonfiction Writers: A Dialogue." *Writing on the Edge* 26, no. 2 (2016): 19–33.

Spotify.Investors. "Spotify Technology S.A. Announces Financial Results for Fourth Quarter 2018." June 2, 2019. https://investors.spotify.com/financials/press-release-details/2019/Spotify-Technology-SA-Announces-Financial-Results-for-Fourth-Quarter-2018/default.aspx.

Stansfield, John and Louise Bunce. "The Relationship between Empathy and Reading Fiction: Separate Roles for Cognitive and Affective Components." *Journal of European Psychology Students* 5, no. 3 (2014): 9–18.

Turvey, Anne, Monica Brady, Abbie Carpenter, and John Yandell. "The Many Voices of the English Classroom." *English in Education*, March 1, 2018. https://www.tandfonline.com/doi/abs/10.1111/j.1754-8845.2006.tb00782.x.

USAFacts. "More than 9 Million Children Lack Internet Access at Home for Online Learning." October 19, 2020. https://usafacts.org/articles/internet-access-students-at-home/.

Vaillant, Derek W. "Sounds of Whiteness: Local Radio, Racial Formation, and Public Culture in Chicago, 1921–1935." *American Quarterly* 54, no. 1 (2002): 25–66.

Vrikki, Photini and Sarita Malik. "Voicing Lived-Experience and Anti-Racism: Podcasting as a Space at the Margins for Subaltern Counterpublics." *Popular Communication* 17, no. 4 (October 2, 2019): 273–87. doi:10.1080/15405702.2019.1622116.

Zuraikat, Laith. "The Parasocial Nature of the Podcast." In *Radio's Second Century: Past, Present, and Future Perspectives*, ed. John Allen Hendricks, 39–52. New Brunswick, NJ: Rutgers University Press, 2020.

Biographies

Saul Lemerond is an assistant professor of Creative Writing and American Literature at Hanover College. His fiction, poetry, and essays have appeared in *Bourbon Penn, Gigantic Sequins, Moon City Review, The Journal of Creative Writing Studies*, and elsewhere.

Leigh Camacho Rourks is an assistant professor of English and Humanities at Beacon College in Central Florida. Her debut story collection, *Moon Trees and Other Orphans*, won the St. Lawrence Book Award. She is also the recipient of the Glenna Luschei Prairie Schooner Award and Robert Watson Literary Review Prize.

Guest Author Biographies

Rebecca Hazelwood teaches Creative Nonfiction at the University of Alabama in Huntsville. Her work has been published or is forthcoming in *Guernica, Passages North, December, Entropy, Anthropoid, Hobart, Still*, and *PANK*.

Kase Johnstun teaches at Saint Joseph Catholic High School. He is the author of *Beyond the Grip of Craniosynostosis: An Inside View of Life Touched by the Congenital Skull Deformity* and *Let the Wild Grasses Grow*. He is the host of the *LITerally Podcast*.

Billie R. Tadros is an assistant professor at The University of Scranton in Scranton, Pennsylvania. She is the author of three books of poems—*Graft Fixation, Was Body*, and *The Tree We Planted and Buried You In*—and three chapbooks—*Am/Are I, inter: burial places*, and *Containers*.

Index